By THOMAS L. QUICK

YOUR ROLE IN TASK FORCE MANAGEMENT (1972)

THE AMBITIOUS WOMAN'S GUIDE TO A SUCCESSFUL CAREER
  (with Margaret V. Higginson, 1975)

UNDERSTANDING PEOPLE AT WORK (1976)

PERSON TO PERSON MANAGING (1977)

THE QUICK MOTIVATION METHOD (1980)

THE PERSUASIVE MANAGER (1982)

BOOSTING EMPLOYEE PERFORMANCE THROUGH BETTER
  MOTIVATION (1983)

EXECUTIVE ASSERTIVENESS (1983)

INCREASING YOUR SALES SUCCESS (1984)

MANAGING PEOPLE AT WORK DESK GUIDE (1984)

THE MANAGER'S MOTIVATION DESK BOOK (1985)

POWER PLAYS (1985)

INSPIRING PEOPLE AT WORK (1986)

QUICK SOLUTIONS (1987)

HOW PEOPLE WORK BEST (1988)

POWER, INFLUENCE AND YOUR EFFECTIVENESS IN HUMAN
  RESOURCES (1988)

MANAGING FOR PEAK PERFORMANCE (1989)

*UN*CONVENTIONAL
WISDOM

Thomas L. Quick

*UN*CONVENTIONAL WISDOM

Irreverent
Solutions
for Tough
Problems
at Work

Jossey-Bass Publishers

San Francisco • Oxford • 1989

650.1
Q 6

*UN*CONVENTIONAL WISDOM
Irreverent Solutions for Tough Problems at Work
   by Thomas L. Quick

Copyright © 1989 by: Jossey-Bass Inc., Publishers
                      350 Sansome Street
                      San Francisco, California 94104
                              &
                      Jossey-Bass Limited
                      Headington Hill Hall
                      London OX3 0BW

Library of Congress Cataloging-in-Publication Data

Quick, Thomas L.
   Unconventional wisdom : irreverent solutions to tough problems at
work / Thomas L. Quick.
      p.   cm.—(The Jossey-Bass management series)
   Includes bibliographical references.
   ISBN 1-55542-177-6
   1. Problem solving.   I. Title.   II. Series.
HD30.29.Q54   1989
650.1—dc20   89-45594
                                                  CIP

Manufactured in the United States of America

The paper in this book meets the guidelines for
permanence and durability of the Committee on
Production Guidelines for Book Longevity of the
Council on Library Resources.

JACKET DESIGN BY WILLI BAUM

FIRST EDITION

Code 8953

The
Jossey-Bass
Management
Series

Contents

Preface

I suspect that the genesis as well as the purpose of this book is best suggested by the title of its first chapter, "Progressing from Certainty to Ambiguity." Many people in management might raise their eyebrows at that declaration of independence, because that indeed is what it is. As a young salesman and manager, I'm sure I was not alone in seeking certainties in whatever I did. After all, the more certain you are about something or someone, the better your decisions, the more self-assured your actions. But certainty, I found as I grew older, brings with it a kind of captivity. If it's this, it certainly can't be that. If it's black, it can't be white. We in America are especially drawn to certainty, primarily because of our puritanical heritage, which stems from the early days of the Church and the Manichaeans: There were two forces, two realities, one good, one evil.

I came to understand that either-or, which characterizes many managerial decisions, is a trap because you have only two boxes in which the whole world must fit. Sometimes, it occurred to me, reality was best defined by both-and. I further discovered that the more options I had, the more possibilities I discovered, and the more successful I was in deciding and solving. And the more fun managing was.

When I was a young editor on the professional staff of the Research Institute of America, my boss, Barbara Whitmore, used to stimulate my thinking by suggesting that I take a given, such as "Managers should delegate," and turn it around to its opposite, "Managers should not delegate." Something interesting might develop on the contrary side. But I was still generating certainties, so I couldn't appreciate what a wonderful door she was opening for me.

But now, having been liberated from the fiction that I must always be factual and absolutely certain, I can cheerfully write about the desirability of a little chaos in your order, laziness in your management, or favoritism in your leadership. Those ideas go against the stereotype and the tradition, but stereotypes and traditions bind and, at my stage in life, I'm seeking more freedom. The key to freedom is choice: The more choices you have, the freer you are. However, the more choices you have, the more ambiguous your situation may be. I've discovered that you simply cannot have freedom without ambiguity.

Some readers may consider my tone to be a bit irreverent. In fact, an early reader of the manuscript suggested that I appeared to be antimanagement. Well, if I poke fun or level criticism at managers and trainers, it's because I've been there. I've been involved with training since 1961 and in management since the late 1960s. I learned management the hardest way possible: In my early years of practicing management I had 100 percent responsibility for the product the department produced and absolutely zero authority over the people who produced it. Later that proportion changed in my favor, but I never lost the value of knowing how to negotiate.

Because I have been both a trainer and a manager in real life, I hope that readers will give me credence. Perhaps some tolerance might be useful, too. This book was written for everyone who is in management or human resources, in any type of organization. These are the audiences I know well. Older managers, I hope, will get a few chuckles as they recognize the validity of some of the examples I have gleaned from my thirty years of organizational life. More senior people may have some of their own life conclusions reinforced by my experiences and observations. Thus encouraged, they may wish to pass on their—our—wisdom to junior managers and human resources specialists. But I would imagine that the greatest amount of learning will be among readers who are still on the ladder and sometimes suspect that what they have been told in the classroom and in textbooks will not always fit with what they see and hear around them. Often in my career as a manager I would express my bafflement by referring to Lewis Carroll: "Which side of the looking glass are we on?"

Unconventional Wisdom expresses my bias. I don't live by much certainty anymore, and I don't much need it. If what I say challenges your assumptions, I suggest that you reexamine both my perceptions and yours and go with whichever one makes you feel more comfortable.

The book is structured in a natural progression, starting with you and your personal effectiveness, then widening the scope to talk about your subordinates, then opening your door so that you can evaluate some of your contacts and transactions with others, and, finally, guiding you to think, possibly in new ways, about your organization—the world in which you must operate.

I spoke earlier about your comfort. I hope that after reading these chapters you'll be as comfortable with ambiguity as I've grown to be. You may even become excited by the prospect of living in a world that is both-and rather than either-or. I further hope that good things happen to you as a result. It's a fantasy of authors that they be allowed to write their own reviews. If I were writing a review of this book, I would suggest that you will find these essays "insightful," "provocative," "thoughtful," and all those wonderful words I have wished that reviewers would say about my books—and on some occasions have. But I guess a word that would be equally valuable to me is "entertaining." It was fun writing this book, and I clearly wish that you have fun reading it.

New York City Thomas L. Quick
August 1989

To Gerald and Mildred

The Author

*T*homas L. Quick has been associated with management training and development for twenty-eight years. For many of those years, he was a member of the professional staff of the Research Institute of America (RIA), supervising the design and production of RIA's sales and management development programs. In 1982, he left RIA to form Resource Strategies Institute, where, as executive director, he writes and edits two monthly newsletters, *Professional Managing* and *Professional Selling*.

An experienced line manager as well as salesman, Quick has written eighteen books and more than five hundred articles, mostly on management methods and leadership skills. His monthly column in *Training News* won the annual Dugan Laird award for distinguished writing on human resources.

He maintains an active private practice in training and organization development consulting in New York City. He is past president of the New York Metro chapter of the American Society for Training and Development.

*UN*CONVENTIONAL WISDOM

Part One

INCREASING YOUR PERSONAL EFFECTIVENESS BY LOSING IT

The English often use the phrase "Tidy it up" to mean that a situation is not quite what it should be and is to be set right. Americans tend "to put things in order" or "to get it under control." All these phrases suggest that there is an appropriate state of things that should be maintained. However, I advise that you develop a bit of disorderliness now and then. "Losing it" points to what I mean, although it implies that this state is not desirable. Well, perhaps we'd all be better off if occasionally we lose it a bit; when we insist upon control, order, and rationality, we often suffer a loss of vision and creativity.

A lot of wonderful things can happen when we abandon the rational standard and let our intuition and emotions ferment. We see options and choices of action that we didn't see before, we discover relationships that we hadn't known existed, and we start asking questions that we hadn't thought to ask previously. At the very least we develop new perspectives on what it means to be not only an effective professional or manager but an effective person as well.

The risk, of course, is untidiness, and that unnerves most people. The purpose of Part One is to encourage you to experiment with untidiness so that you can benefit from the increased opportunity and effectiveness untidiness engenders. Get more comfortable with chaos and ambiguity—that's where most of the fun and adventure are. Depending almost constantly on the logical and analytical side of the brain gets boring after a while.

1

Chapter 1

Progressing from Certainty to Ambiguity

I was, I think, in my forties before I learned that decisiveness is not necessarily related to good decision making. All the corporate executives who were supposed to be, by virtue of their publicity, models for us were described as, among other things, decisive. They were fast on their feet. Some of them no doubt resembled Harry Truman in that, after a difficult decision, they slept soundly that night.

But decisiveness, as I came to understand it, demanded speed of action, not always soundness of judgment. In fact, one of the executives in a company that employed me made very fast and firm decisions that sometimes proved less than wise at best, disastrous at worst. I'm quite sure that a similar phenomenon is readily observable in most other organizations managed by decisive people.

Why then are the characteristics associated with the word *decisive* so admired, and why does its antonym, *indecisive,* arouse such scorn? To say that someone is indecisive is to portray him or her as weak, vacillating, and wimpy. And to use a similar word, *ambiguous,* is to suggest untrustworthiness. In fact, in both cases, we might simply be talking about a person who has not yet made up his or her mind. Why is it considered not virtuous to take time to make a decision, or, heaven forbid, in some cases not to make one at all?

I suspect that the reason we distrust indecisiveness and ambiguity lies in our puritan heritage with its Manichaean roots. The Manichaeans were dualists: Good and evil principles existed side by side. God is in His heaven and Satan is in his hell. And if you weren't claimed by God, you'd be the possession of the devil. Our puritan forefathers adopted this either-or perspective: good or

3

evil, black or white, right or wrong. Today, even though we don't see ourselves as practicing puritans, we still seem to have an aversion to anything that isn't either-or. We have a lot of trouble with shades of gray.

The late Alfred P. Sloan, Jr., the chairman of General Motors who built the corporation that we know, seemed to recognize this problem. If a group or committee he chaired came to a firm agreement on an issue, he would ask, "Then, are you all agreed that we should go ahead on this?" When heads nodded around the table, he'd reply, "All right, we'll adjourn this meeting until someone can come up with a reason why we shouldn't."

Ours is, I fear, a compulsively solution-oriented society that is uncomfortable taking time with problems. Suppose you say to a friend, "I have this annoying headache." His retort might be "Take Tylenol. It always works for me." Note that he doesn't seem interested where in your head the pain is or how long you've had it. His role, as he sees it, is not to explore the problem with you but to find a solution.

"I have taken something for it," you protest, somewhat annoyed that he might believe you are too dumb to know there are antidotes for pain. After all, you've watched that pedantic woman on television tell you, just as your third grade teacher did, that you may think you know about painkillers, but you really don't. "What concerns me is that it is a recurring headache."

"Well, then," your friend advises, somewhat impatiently, "you should see a doctor." Not only is the advice superfluous, but you are beginning to suspect that your friend has a very low estimate of your intelligence.

"I have seen my doctor. He's puzzled. My headaches come and go."

"Perhaps you should see a specialist."

"I'm starting to realize that they come and go after I've eaten sardines."

Now it's apparent that you may have an interesting allergy, a problem that should be explored. But in order to talk about what you've discovered, you had to climb over all the barriers that your friend erected trying to find a solution for you.

Sometimes the problem you have is benign, challenging,

interesting, and even fun to work through. Once, after a talk by consultant Peter Block, I started wondering whether freedom was an issue for me, as he had suggested it might be for a number of people in the audience. Do I have as much freedom in my life as I think I do? As much as I want? Intrigued, I discussed these issues with a friend, who immediately broke in and said, "I don't think you do." That was the end of my thinking out loud with him. I tried the process with another friend, who listened quietly and impassively. When I paused, she took out a card and said, "I really think you ought to talk to my shrink. Here's his number."

My friends' aversion to the unresolved, the uncertain, and the ambiguous took the fun out of noodling through a philosophical, perhaps existential, problem. So henceforth I'll do that noodling alone. But my friends share their aversion with a large proportion of the population, and when that aversion interferes with good decision making, the result could be more than annoyance: It could be costly.

I remember one occasion when I was asked to sit in on what I thought was to be a discussion of a proposed project for the field sales force in my company. I listened to the presentation and, since the plan did not seem to me to be workable in its original form, I suggested some changes. There was an embarrassed silence; then one of the plan's proponents angrily declared that *he* thought it was quite acceptable and would we please vote on it. I was a pariah—I had introduced uncertainty. There were further discussions about the plan, but I was conspicuously excluded from them. Implementation of the plan, as I recall, was an expensive failure.

I did not see myself as a troublemaker; rather, I was suggesting some options, and options are what decision making is all about. I cannot decide my existential question of freedom while in a vacuum. The options I develop in my ruminating will determine how much freedom I have. The more options I have, the greater is my freedom. The more people involved, the more options might be uncovered. And in fact, in any decision making, the more options that can be developed, the sounder the decision is likely to be.

Taking time to develop options and choices is the essence of good decision making, and that's why I universally favor consensus decisions when more than one decision maker is involved. Consensus is not a terribly popular process in the American corporation, not only because it takes longer, but because those involved in it are uncomfortable having to spend time with uncertainty and ambiguity. This discomfort explains why there is often a tendency for the group to go with the first seemingly feasible option. Count on it: There will be someone who will say, "Well, are we agreed? Let's vote." Sloan knew the phenomenon and the temptation.

When compared to a brisk discussion and a fast vote, arriving at a consensus seems messy. People talk in and around and through issues and sometimes miss them altogether. It's important that the leadership exercise some control over where the discussion is going without censoring it. Unless people in the group have been members of successful consensus decision-making groups, they are likely to become quite uncomfortable during this seemingly free-flowing phase. There is the urge for closure—on something, maybe even on anything. There may be an attempt at control by the I-think-we're-off-the-subject intervention. It takes wise and patient direction in this early stage. The ambiguity, the uncertainty, and the lack of resolution drive some people to demand firm action and a definite decision, often prematurely.

In consensus decision making, positives play a much more important role than do the negatives. The nay-sayer is not, in such a group, regarded as a savior, as he or she might be in a different, less mature group. Leadership sets the tone by encouraging positive opinions and areas of agreement. Periodically the areas in which there is agreement are defined and summarized. The group has the feeling that it is making progress as the various members move closer together. Even so, it often takes courage for the leader to resist the pressure to close. Instead, he or she should ask, "Are we sure we've considered all the options available to us?"

A consensus decision is a sculpted, almost artistic creation. First, there is the formless raw material. A shape begins to emerge from the kneading and pressing. Angles change. This is added; that is taken away. Narrow this part; widen that. Shrink. Expand. And finally, everyone stands back in admiration with a bit of surprise that all the effort has actually produced something that everyone believes is the best of all the options. People don't just go along, as is so often true in a majority decision. They join wholeheartedly in supporting the finished product.

I've become so comfortable with ambiguity that when I hear someone say, "Well, the answer is either this or that," I suspect that a bad decision is about to be made. Looking back on my own life, I'm curious about how one becomes comfortable with ambiguity, with uncertainty, or with the need to be firmly planted on one side of the fence. Age perhaps is a factor. A friend reminded me the other day about how pompous we were when we were in our twenties and thirties. We'd argue for hours to prove our positions. There was only one way to believe, one way to do things. Somewhere along the line you realize that, no, there can be more than one way to believe, more than one way to do things. In fact, I now find it useful, in thinking through a problem, to argue at least two sides of the issue.

I discovered a few years ago during a management workshop on motivation that there is more than one way to believe. I had been lecturing on feedback, and I said negative feedback should be kept separate from positive, if possible. But in no case should praise precede criticism. An elderly gentleman raised his hand and commented that he did it quite successfully. So, graciously, I thought, I asked him to explain how he combined the positive with the negative, figuring that I'd have no problem rebutting his example. He recounted the problem behavior of a key employee and how he had called that key employee into his office, and said, "If I didn't think that you are a valuable asset to this operation, I wouldn't take the time to tell you what I'm about to tell you about your performance."

I instantly became a convert to more ambiguity. About the same time, too, I was getting some unpleasant evaluations of my training sessions, probably because I was conveying so much certainty in my responses to questions from managers. I doubt that I felt I was totally in the right, but undoubtedly more and more participants in my workshops were hearing, "This is right. That is wrong." Some unpleasant words began to show up on the smile sheets: arrogant, egotistic, overbearing. I learned something valuable about myself.

Now, before my speeches and workshops, I make a little announcement that goes something like this: "What you'll hear today is totally my bias. I'm beyond the Moses complex. It got a little tiring carrying all those stone tablets around. Besides, God doesn't talk much to me these days, especially about managing. The beauty part of the bias is that you can feel free to accept it in whole or just in part, to argue with it, to reject it, or to question it. So feel free."

Another favorite phrase of mine, left over from junior philosophy, is, "All generalizations are false, including this one." I can't remember its source, but I'm quite sure the Jesuits didn't teach it to me.

And so far as decision making goes, I'm an adherent of the Scarlett O'Hara method: I'll think about it tomorrow—or next week. I like to stay firmly on all sides of a question until my intuition tells me what I should do. Almost invariably it does, and during the time I'm waiting, I have a chance to think about all the various options. My intuition will point out the right one to me. It's much smarter than my conscious intelligence; because it has been through so much with me, it knows me, and it has been enriched by the wisdom of others whom I have admired. But my intuition has a soft voice, and I must lower my own to listen.

I have in fact become so comfortable with ambiguity that I have come to distrust certainty. The other night I watched a high-level government bureaucrat on television talk about how his agency was solving the problem of the increasing insolvency of savings and loan institutions. It's a subject that I have followed in the business press, and I have some idea of the complexity of the problem. Yet, despite the tough questions he got from the interviewer, the official gave crisp, definite answers, and came across as very self-assured. I concluded that no one was entitled to be that certain about such an uncertain future. He made me very uncomfortable.

If I had a message for the publicists in our corporations, it would be this: Opt for ambiguity every time. For example, a defense contractor has been caught with its fingers in the government till. The company puts out an announcement: "X Corporation has always abided by the highest ethical principles, and under no circumstances would we tolerate any fraud involving government funds. Therefore, despite the accusations produced by the two-year investigation by the FBI, we can state categorically that these charges are baseless. The integrity of X Corporation is intact."

Well, of course, that's a statement of certainty. The problem is that no one really believes it. It's better to be a bit ambiguous: "The X Corporation is grieved to hear these serious charges and wishes to announce that, while it does not have proof of wrongdoing, it will not tolerate any misuse of government funds. If our investigation uncovers fraud, the practice will be stopped and the people involved punished." Then X Corporation fires its CEO, and some confidence is restored. The lawyers may not like it, but, come to think of it, lawyers themselves are great at being ambiguous.

I recognize that leadership and decisiveness often go together in people's minds, but a leader should be measured by the validity of his or her decisions, not by the speed with which they are made.

I suppose most of us dislike ambiguity because of our mothers. Remember when you were a kid and asked your mother for something? She'd say, "We'll see." That was ambiguous. Or it seemed to be. In fact, as you grew older, you realized that she had already made up her mind. She didn't want the hassle that would follow her telling you no.

We've all been scarred by ambiguity.

Chapter 2

Putting Some Chaos
in Your Order

*A*t long last, I admit my schizophrenia. Part of me craves structure while another part occasionally seeks chaos, although perhaps not as often as it should for my total mental health.

I not only crave structure, I'm a structure freak. When I get up most mornings, I have a fairly clear idea of how I will spend the day. After my hour with The *New York Times* comes the twenty minutes on the exercycle and then breakfast. I'm usually at the typewriter by eight with a goal of four manuscript pages by ten or so, when I check on the mail. Another four pages by noon, and it's time to break for lunch. And so on, for the rest of the day. At the beginning of the month, I often know how I shall be spending the rest of it. In fact, I have a clear schedule of what I'll be doing ten months into the future. That supposedly is the portrait of an effective person.

Yet, I identify with the famous scene from the W. C. Fields movie in which Fields, sitting in an office before a rolltop desk whose drawers and pigeonholes are crammed with papers, is asked for a particular document. Muttering to himself, he surveys the mess before him, then says, "Here it is," reaches into a pile, and extracts the desired piece of paper. As I recall, there was a horrified gasp from the audience before a wave of laughter, demonstrating that, as someone said, the essence of humor is incongruity.

I not only identify with that scene, I cherish it, because of my anarchic side—my rebellious self. There are times when even obsessive structuralists like me have to admit that too much of a good thing may do damage to the soul—times when I have to deal with the anxiety of simply floating free of a schedule or a system. Like Fields, I sometimes let piles of paper grow, and as long as I know what's in each of them, I can usually control my tension. But when I unsuccessfully look in one pile for something that is in another, my obsession reasserts itself. I must have structure.

Abraham Maslow asserts that the need for structure is basic. He places it below safety needs and just above physiological needs on his hierarchy. But how healthy is it when, getting up on a morning in which I have no schedule, I pace the floor tensely, desperately seeking something I should be doing? I know exactly what the anthropologist Konrad Lorenz felt when, after years of taking one route into Vienna and another route home, he experimented briefly with reversing the routes—the exit as entrance and the entrance as exit. By briefly I mean once. The anxiety caused by the departure from routine practice overwhelmed him.

One of the beneficial consequences of writing books is that there is a need to free-associate. At least, I feel the need. I realize that the first commandment of good writing is "Start with an outline." But I've broken that commandment a number of times, along with some of the other ten. The conceptual time for a book is time for chaos. In fact, for a book, a speech, an article, or even a paragraph— especially a brief paragraph—there is a need for cross-fertilization. *Lateral association* is another name for the process.

Making an outline perpetuates the compartmentalized way most of us have been taught all of our lives. We learn in boxes. When we generate ideas in that tradition, we do not use our imaginations. We construct our boxes, as we have been taught to do. If the idea fits the box—what we already know—we include it. If it doesn't, we ignore or dismiss it.

My definition of creativity is seeing relationships that we didn't know existed. We have to tear down the walls of the boxes so ideas can flow across and back and forth. Of course, when we do that, we risk creating some chaos—no more safe little boxes to store ideas and no more self-imposed boundaries to restrict our thinking. It's tension producing, and you can see just how much by observing a class on business writing. Trainees usually have exercises to do, and in my groups, I time the exercises. Most trainees begin to write the second the instructor says to start. Judging by what and how they write, I can only conclude that most of them don't know what they will put down on paper but that seeing something emerge on the paper is pacifying. Thinking it through first seems too formidable a process.

Indulge me while I digress slightly. I'll be bold enough to say that there is no good writing without thinking. That is, good writing is good thinking. Clear writing is clear thinking. Teaching people the principles and mechanics of writing is not enough; we must teach them to think. If I am right in my premise, then I have some dismal news: Relatively few people in our society have learned how to think analytically and logically. For years, I have asked the participants in my writing classes to construct a paragraph from a lead sentence such as, "When I write well, I am more effective." Despite the two keys that can be developed—*write well* and *effective*—most trainees are unable to develop a logical, sequential flow. That's not because they're not writers; it's because they cannot think their way from A to B to C in a straight line. I am extremely pessimistic about the significant long-term advantages of trying to teach people writing skills in a day or two. If you want to change the way people express themselves on paper, you need time enough to teach them the rudiments of the rational process. And that's not possible in two days.

Incidentally, a revealing behavior by trainees in writing classes is the tendency to do the exercises single-spaced. A professional would double-space, because he or she would recognize both the need and the desirability of revision and editing. But either the trainees do not see their essays as a creative effort or the blank spaces that suggest changes are threatening.

Conception time is for me the most exciting stage in writing anything. I sit down with a yellow pad (a fact that provoked one writing trainee to suggest that the reason the members of the class weren't doing well on their exercises was that they were using white pads). Chaos doesn't come easily, however. Sometimes I assist it with a glass of wine, although the role of alcohol is strictly limited to this initial stage. My favorite bartender once asked me whether booze helped the writing, and I responded that booze doesn't help much of anything.

I'll start with the overall theme; let's say, power. (I did a book on the subject of power in organizations in 1985.) I write down everything that comes to mind. There is no formatting, no organizing, and no censoring at this point. I draw on what I've read about power, how I've seen it used and abused in my thirty years of organizational life, and what people seem to perceive about power—their biases and fears, its good and bad aspects. After many days, I have page after page of notes. Now it's time to look for relationships and similarities. Some notes have to do with types or sources of power, others with the exercise of power with subordinates, or with peers, or with higher management. Each category represents a potential chapter of the book. It's almost as if the material has shaped itself. I have not consciously imposed a progression or an order on it. I have simply abandoned myself to my thought and creative processes. Thought will produce concepts, facts, and perceptions, and creativity will link them. The processes include both vertical and lateral thinking as well as intuiting and sensing.

Introducing chaos is not without risk. You worry about how much you can come up with. (I'm always surprised to find that I know much more about a subject than I thought I did when I started.) It's sloppy, and at the end of each session with yourself, you have only pages on which you've scrawled very raw thoughts to show for your labor. You may even fear that there will be no end, that you will simply make notes forever. But your notes will show you that you've pretty well mined the shaft when you start repeating yourself. When most of the notes seem to be slightly different versions of previous entries, then it's time to categorize.

Repetition is the key to closing down the chaos that often exists in group problem solving and decision making. Sometimes it's difficult to, as they say, get people's arms around a problem, and there may seem to be aimless talking and circular deliberation—people winding up where they started. An astute group leader may let this go on for a time, but when people start to repeat themselves or one another, the leader knows it is time to intervene.

Unfortunately, many group leaders structure their meetings to allow little time for chaos. I've had two experiences recently that caused me no end of frustration, because I believed the group leaders were so uncomfortable at the seemingly chaotic discussion that they closed off the opportunities for truly creative decisions. In the first, the group was made up of distinguished professionals deliberating on a problem that was cosmically vague. Each member was contributing his or her perception of the nature of the problem, trying to find some common ground on which we could build a resolution. The chairman seemed to fret about the aimlessness of the talk, and two or three times he said, "I hope we're finished with all this venting." In my usual manner, I silently applauded the chaos and regretted his value judgment: venting has a negative connotation.

In another case, our task force had settled down to do some casual searching of options. We had the time and the inclination. But the chair was impatient. Seizing upon the first suggestion, she took over the meeting. Standing by the flip chart, marker in hand, she demanded, "How are we going to make this work? We need an action plan." We caved in under the fierce direction. We dutifully developed an action plan, which, some months later, proved to be unworkable. To our credit, however, the next morning the task force members held a postmortem in which some lamented the loss of our freedom—and our chaos.

Examples like these are legion. They go on in every kind of organization. We must have order. We must have structure. We must have full agendas. If we're not producing plans and solutions, we are not working. That's one of the discomforts that you might experience in writing according to my method—for some time, you'll have only scrawled notes to show that you've done anything.

When people seem directionless, they seem to be floundering. And floundering has a weak image—certainly not the accepted characteristic of the person who is in charge of the situation. But I've found that floundering well takes strong people. And for people who believe that chaos is a state to avoid at all costs, remember that before God brought order out of chaos, He first created chaos. It gave Him more possibilities.

Chapter 3

You Need to Sell Well
to Perform Well

*O*ne of the most successful seminars ever marketed was "Finance for the Nonfinancial Manager." But I have a fantasy that, in the 1990s, its success will be rivaled by a seminar called "Selling for the Nonsales Person." (I suspect that anyone marketing that program can come up with a better title.) There's a fabulous market out there—almost everyone. The late Red Motley, publisher of *Parade* magazine, used to say that "Nothing happens until somebody sells something." What a profound truth. The fact is, everyone is selling constantly, although people don't realize that they are selling, and many of them don't do it very well. They need a lot of help. And the person who finds a way to merchandise that help successfully is going to make a lot of money.

I thought I was going to make a lot of money back in the early 1980s when I realized that for years I had been counseling managers in techniques that would make them more effective—techniques based on the selling skills I had learned as a salesman. Well, I thought, I'll write a book showing people how they can get more of what they want from other people using basic sales skills. *The Persuasive Manager* came out in 1982 and sold about 8,000 copies before disappearing. Managers strongly resist the idea that they sell, and their resistance works to their disadvantage.

Recently I was asked to conduct sales skills workshops for some people who also usually don't see themselves as selling anything—insurance loss control specialists, nuclear chemists, and nuclear power engineers. In all cases, their managements had determined that training these folks in sales techniques would improve not only their persuasive talents but also their everyday communication abilities. Okay, I said to myself, the long-awaited bonanza begins.

Well, not quite. There's nothing wrong with my premise that everyone can benefit from knowing how to use selling skills to persuade others. But people have a hard time accepting it because, as I've mentioned, they resist the idea of selling. Apparently the negative stereotype of a salesperson is stubborn and pervasive. And that's unfortunate, because in my thirty-five years or so of observing people in organizations, I've concluded beyond question that the people who get things done and who are most effective in getting the results they want are those with superb selling skills.

I have identified eight characteristics of influential people I've known. First, they know what they want. When they're in a transaction of some sort, if only a chat, they have a good idea of what they'd like to happen as a result of it—an opinion, support, some other action or behavior in the other person. Influential people have a win-oriented mentality, although the really successful ones know that the best transaction is one in which everyone comes away with something. People who operate on a win-lose basis eventually experience resistance from others.

Second, they know they have a right to get what they want. No one has a right to get what he or she wants, but influential people know they have a right to try—an attitude many people don't share. I have a dear friend who has a responsible job on Wall Street. She likes to read The *Wall Street Journal,* but she has to retrieve copies from others. "Ask for your own," I've urged her. Her answer: "No, they won't agree." It drives me crazy. In fact, I often advise managers to ask for things, even when they suspect the answer will be no. The mere asking creates visibility and conveys a confident opinion of oneself.

Third, they are articulate. Influential people stand out because they express themselves in a logical, concise, sequential, attractive manner. I say attractive because they make it easy for people to follow and to understand. I have observed that articulateness is not necessarily equated with intelligence. Some politicians and CEOs are remarkably expressive, yet they do very stupid things. Ironically people often respond favorably to someone who makes his or her position clear, even if it is dumb.

Fourth, influential individuals are sensitive. They know how to read others to divine their wants and needs. They understand that if you are to give those others what they need and want—an essential in selling—you must first know what those things are. Influential people are also sensitive to the most appropriate time and place to approach others with their ideas or proposals.

Fifth, they are credible. They subscribe to what I call the Nathan Hale principle: "I only regret that I have but one credibility to lose." If they lose it, they've hanged themselves. They work very hard to build their believability and trustworthiness, because without it, they offer little reason for anyone to do what they wish. I wish managers understood how fragile credibility is and how important it is to their effectiveness.

Sixth, influential people know how to deal with opposition. Someday this subject will be an important segment of management training as it is in sales, because most people don't know how to cope with resistance. What happens to you when you advance that lovely little idea and someone suggests that it won't work? Do you smile and relax? Or do you get red in the face and sputter and try to argue your opponent down? Watch an influential person operate. He or she doesn't look defensive. Instead, the pro relaxes, listens, decides on the right moment to rebut—or whether to do so at all. The influential person seems always in control, even when he or she is in a tight spot.

Seventh, they know how to ask for the action they want. The Agatha Christie school of communicating (hang on long enough and you'll figure out the mystery of what I want from you) is not for them. They let you know quickly what they'd like from you, because they want you to listen to the reasons you should agree; they don't want you to sit there impatiently trying to unravel the mystery. Of course, one reason people delay asking for action is that they're afraid, as salespeople are, of rejection. But the influential individual has confidence in his or her support for the proposal. He or she is reasonably sure that you'll sit there and listen, simply because it makes sense for you to do so.

And eighth, influential people know what motivates others. When they advance ideas or suggestions, they know it isn't enough to know what they want to sell, and they know it's essential to match what they are selling to what others would like to buy. So, in advancing a proposal, they make it interesting; they make it valuable; they make it easy for the other person.

Such are the characteristics of influential people I've been able to identify through the years. But how do they sell? They sell themselves and their ideas exactly as salespeople sell products, services, and programs. When I look at the selling process I knew as a salesman, I see five steps essential to persuading others: (1) Know your product, (2) know your prospect, (3) involve your prospect, (4) ask for action, and (5) be prepared to handle opposition. Let's take a closer look at each step.

Know Your Product. I ask any audience that is listening to me expound upon these steps, "What is your product?" Their answers include ideas, planning, training, projects, and themselves. Perhaps. The most effective salesperson, and concomitantly the successful influential individual, goes beyond this level. What is the ultimate product? It exists in the prospect's mind, usually. For example, the insurance loss control representative visits the insured's place of business and sees a tank that has a potentially dangerous valve on it. The rep suggests to the insured that he invest in a new, safer valve. The insured protests that the tank hasn't leaked in the ten years the valve has been on it. Well, that would seem to be the end of the sale of the valve. But the influential person knows clearly that he or she is not selling a valve. Even though there has been no leakage in ten years, the influential individual knows that the possibility exists and that in the back of the insured's mind is the realization that it could happen.

The salesperson's approach goes something like this: "From my tour of the plant, Mr. Jones, and from talking with some of your people, I realize that their safety is an important consideration for you. It's true that the valve hasn't leaked in ten years, and you may be right that it won't. And you may not be right. From what I've come to know about you today, I'm convinced that if something happened, and there were a leak, and they carried one of your employees out of here on a stretcher, you'd be very upset and worried. And you'd probably say to yourself, 'Why didn't I change that valve?' "

The salesperson is not selling a valve or a recommendation.

Instead, he or she is selling peace of mind—security. How can the insured sleep a bit better at night? As I say to training audiences, "You're not selling your training program. You're selling increased effectiveness, better performance, bigger profits."

Know Your Prospect. With a bit of imagination, most people can figure out the product they're selling. They can identify their needs and wants. But how about the prospect's needs and wants? If you're not selling what the prospect wants to buy, you're talking to the wall. In many of my workshops, I demonstrate that most of us are quite weak in exploring the prospect's needs. We just don't take the time and effort to find out what their needs are. After all, our thinking goes, what we sell makes so much sense there's simply no way the prospect can refuse to say yes.

My means of demonstration is a little exercise based on the following scenario: You are a department head who has been asked to lead a task force to study the adoption of flextime by your organization and make recommendations for its design and administration. Your mandate has been given to you by a vice president who has suggested that certain personnel be members of the task force. However, the actual recruiting has been left to you. You have little difficulty persuading most other managers on your level to lend you key people for your part-time task force, which you estimate will require an average of two hours' participation per week for several weeks. There is one prospective member, a statistical analyst, whom you want to recruit but whose boss so far has been reluctant to grant release time. The boss of the analyst is, in theory, equal to you, but, in fact, she is highly regarded by management and considered by her peers, including you, to be on the fast track. She has achieved high visibility and much autonomy in her department.

"How," I ask the trainees in my workshops, "will you persuade her to let you have the person you want?" One frequent answer is, "Tell her how important this project is to the company." In short, ask where her loyalty is. Others suggest trying what they think is tact: "All of the other managers have cooperated; I'm sure you'll want to." In other words, ask whether she wants to be known as someone who isn't a team player. And then there's the threat: "I'll just have to report back to the vice president that I couldn't persuade you to let your subordinate join us." And she'll get punished for being a bad girl.

Few participants ever seem to realize that the woman is probably playing a power game. Her attitude is, "I have something you want; what are you going to give me for it?" The trainees simply don't think in terms of negotiating, such as, "I'm sure, Ms. Fasttrack, that you would want to have some say in a decision that is going to affect you." Of course, she would. She's a controlling person. She doesn't want to be left out. There are other sales pitches, such as increased visibility for her subordinate and for herself, glory, and so on. These are her needs and wants, and many of us just are not conscious of the necessity to try to understand what the needs are and then to sell to them.

Involve Your Prospect. Quite simply, involving your prospect means matching what you have to sell with what the other person would like to buy by using language that I demonstrated in the previous paragraph. If she wants control, and that's what you have to offer, great. You may have a sale. If the prospect wants peace of mind or the assurance of security or comfort, that's how you slant your presentation. Much of selling means reinforcing a person's image of himself or herself as authoritative, considerate, thoughtful, prudent, and so forth. Anytime you can provide, through what you have to offer, a means to bolster the person's self-image, you are well on the way to making a sale.

Salespeople often involve a prospect by asking questions about the person's needs or perspectives on the operation. Questioning implies that he or she is an equal in the transaction—a partner. By questioning, you're honoring him or her. Establish partnerships, because when you are in such a mode, you assume that the other person brings strengths, wants, needs, and resources to the transaction. And those characteristics combined with your own can point to a solution or benefit to both of you.

Ask for Action. When you state what you'd like in the beginning, up front and confidently, you convey the message that what you're asking is the most natural thing in the world. It's what salespeople call being assumptive. You assume that you have every right to be asking for and getting what you want. When you come across so positively and self-assuredly, you influence the other person. I always recommend that words represented by the acronym *KEY* form the basis for any presentation you make to another, no matter how informal. *K* stands for the key point. An example illustrates its importance: One woman in a business writing course I gave was asked to write a memo presenting a solution to a problem in her office. She wrote five paragraphs describing the problem and only one paragraph suggesting a solution. That one paragraph should have been in the beginning of the letter; it was most important, and nothing should have taken the spotlight off it. *E* is the explanation or elaboration to show why you consider what went first to be the main point or recommendation. And finally, *Y* is for windup (get it?). In selling, it goes like this: "I've told you what to do, why you should do it, and in my windup, I'm going to tell you how to do it as easily as possible." Remember: Make it interesting; make it valuable; make it easy.

Be Prepared to Handle Opposition. To the person who is not trained in selling, focusing on possible opposition could be dangerous because he or she can get so primed in what could go wrong that defensiveness is a sure thing when something does go wrong. Or, as in the case of a novice salesperson, the presentation could get so loaded with answers to potential objections that it doesn't present a positive point of view. After all, you don't want to suggest possible objections or reservations to people you want to influence. At the same time, you'd better be prepared to deal with their hesitation, objections, or arguments.

Too many people see selling as an intellectual exchange of information or as a rational process. Their attitude is, "If I give you all the facts, you'll make your mind up the right way." They may try to let the facts speak for themselves, but facts seldom speak for themselves. You must speak for them. You must present your arguments in such a way that the person sitting across from you understands what you want and is persuaded to give it to you. The decision-making process is not only rational but intuitive, psychological, and emotional. And, if you are to be a successful influencer, you must be prepared to be effective on all levels.

Back in my Gestalt days, with its emphasis on here and now, I came up with four questions that you might ask during a transaction to keep you on your path to the result you want: (1) What do I want from this transaction? (2) What do I think the other person would like? (3) What is going on at this moment? (4) How does this interaction help us both to get what we want?

Keeping those questions and the selling process in mind as you deal with your boss, your client, your co-workers, or your employees will enhance the possibility that you will get what you want from them. Remember Red Motley's wisdom: "Nothing happens until somebody sells something." That includes you, although, like most people, you probably didn't see yourself as a salesperson.

You are.

Chapter 4

Justifying Laziness as a Managerial Virtue

*S*ome of the best managers I've known were lazy, an observation that defies the stereotype. I've always suspected that's one of the reasons why they were good at managing. When you work for them, you know you have a lot of room in which to do what you are skilled at, to do what you most like to do, and to do what it takes for you to grow. The lazy manager generally has his or her eye on results, not on activity, knowing that if the results are good in the department, the manager shines no matter who was primarily responsible for achieving them.

Keeping an eye on what departmental activity produces rather than on the activity itself is not commonplace in American business. There seems to be a fascination with being busy or at least with being seen as busy. Michael Korda, in his famous book *Power,* suggested that a full appointment book confers power on its owner. I've always thought that a jammed schedule rather suggests that its possessor has lost control of his or her life. Ironically, a busy schedule is a controlling device. The person who crams something into every minute can avoid having to deal with people and issues that might pose a problem or a challenge. But that is getting more pathological than I intended to get when I started this.

The stereotype of the successful person is busyness, not laziness. A current ad shows just such a person. The voice-over is that of the wife who talks about how her husband gets plenty of exercise, eats the right foods, and in general takes good care of himself. He is shown having conferences on the run in the corridor, running up stairs rather than taking the elevator, having a snack of an apple while in a stand-up meeting. It's exhausting simply to watch it. But the stereotype is not restricted to executives. A few years ago, an ad series portrayed the so-called New York woman. I forget the product, but the ad made an indelible impression on me. Everywhere she went, she went at a breakneck speed. To save time, presumably, she parked her glasses in her hair. She didn't hail a cab from the sidewalk, she charged into the street and practically pulled the cab to a stop. While I realize that the pace of life in New York City is faster than it is in Kankakee, I protest that those of us who live in Manhattan are not all so driven. For years after, incidentally, I had a bias against people who wore their glasses on top of their heads when they weren't using them. Perhaps I objected to the way they were using them to convey a message.

The stereotype of the frantic, rushed executive is not just a product of Madison Avenue. Read the profiles of managers and specialists on the fast track that appear in the business press. They get along on three hours of sleep each night, are at their desks at five in the morning, go back after dinner, see their families once or twice a year, spend months at a time on airplanes, and are all thin because they have no time for breakfast or lunch. Dinner is probably a roll and a salad. It's all very tiresome—and tiring.

You're surely getting the message that I am not impressed with such frenetic activity. I've had bosses who were always on the go, but who never seemed to accomplish anything once they got where they were going. And I've had other bosses who were possessed by their particular demons and who seemed to believe that working seven days a week was the Protestant ethic.

All well and good, my devil's advocate says, but lazy people don't accomplish much. If you don't invest the time and effort that the busy people do, you can't hope to get much done. Wrong, I reply. I shall have the temerity to suggest that smart lazy people have more worthwhile values than the stereotypes I've been describing—and pillorying. Lazy people are more likely to concentrate on achievement. Perhaps even more to the point, they focus on achieving what is important to achieve. They are rarities in our society, which admires busyness. They know the difference between being efficient and being effective. Peter Drucker has been known to draw the distinction as follows: Being efficient means doing things right, and being effective means doing the right things. I refer to efficiency as the input and effectiveness as the output. Since lazy people can't trumpet their activity, they must emphasize results. Very healthy.

If you would be lazy, goes the old German proverb, you must not be dumb. It's necessary to distinguish between smart lazy people and just plain lazy folks who don't care whether anything gets finished. Naturally, being lazy myself, I talk only about smart lazy people. I've not been accused of being dumb. Stupid at times, yes, but not dumb.

I suspect the issue of laziness became important for me just about the time the term *midlife crisis* became popular. I truly am a child of my times because when people started to talk about restlessness and frustration and life's meaning and burnout, I was approaching my midforties—just the time when males begin to question what it has all been about. (Females generally suffer their midlife crises starting about thirty-five or a bit later—much earlier than men. I don't know why. It may have something to do with the biological clock.)

As is true with so many other men, I began to look at my life. I had a responsible, interesting job that I was happy to get out of bed for on Monday mornings. I was doing the kind of work I loved—writing and editing. The pay was good. The corporate culture was superb. There was plenty of opportunity for me to grow. Yet, I looked on all of this as an input. What about the results of all of it? Money? Yes. Fame? Not really, because at the Research Institute of American (RIA) we didn't have bylines. Satisfaction? Yes. Freedom? There's the sticking point. Freedom means having lots of options. The freer you are, the more options you have. I wanted options. I wanted to do the kind of work I wanted to do and to have it credited to me. As a consequence of all that questioning, I now have my own practice in consulting and training, and I write books. I do what I want to do when I want to do it—and only as much as I want to do.

But there was another and more immediate consequence that affected my management style. I began to appreciate the value of doing what I wanted to do, given the constraints of organizational life, in which no one is very free. I realized the truth of an important management principle: Managers should do only what they have to do as managers. That principle escapes many practitioners of management who often seem to believe that they must be prepared and able to do not only their managerial tasks but also those of everyone else who reports to them.

From that moment of realization, I was a convert to laziness. I resolved to do what I thought a manager should do and let my associates do what they wanted to do and what they were capable of doing. If they weren't capable of doing what I thought they should do, then another responsibility of mine was to help them be capable.

I won't say that my conversion was altogether painless. One of the reasons why managers wind up doing their own and other people's work is that when they are promoted, they take the choicest tasks with them. They want to continue doing what they enjoyed at a lower level. One of the toughest recommendations to make to a manager is: Don't delegate what you don't want to do; delegate what you *do* want to do. In many cases, that will be what the manager shouldn't be doing. I therefore had to get rid of some of the editorial and writing duties that I liked. And as a manager I had to take on other editorial duties I wasn't fond of.

Another inhibitor to delegating is the realization that if a job gets screwed up, the manager is "it." The tail gets pinned on the manager's donkey. Many managers decide that it is the lesser of two evils to do it all themselves. When I was promoted, I was not tempted. By that time I had a taste of the freedom that laziness brought, and I determined the risk was worth it. Besides, remembering the German proverb, I realized that one has to be smart about letting go of a task. You have to know where it goes and what people are doing with it. Although I was lazy, I knew better than to relax too much.

In my case the most important and enjoyable benefit of laziness was the thinking time. I could put my feet on my desk and just read—magazines, books, and journals. I was fortunate to have an enlightened boss who believed that everything was grist for the RIA editor's mill. I looked for new concepts and trends that might prove useful to our subscribers. I searched for new specialties that my subordinates might get interested in. Sometimes I just thought about how good our products were, how we might make them better, and what new products we should experiment with. And I thought about my subordinates and what kinds of tasks would give them a sense of growth or satisfaction.

I didn't believe that thinking time was a luxury. I assumed it was an essential part of the manager's job. But many managers tell me that thinking time for them is rare. In some cases it's because they busy themselves with activity, some of which, as I've pointed out, they probably shouldn't be doing. But in other cases, managers who take time out to read and to think are criticized for not being busy. Consequently, the thinking and reading these managers do are on their own time, away from the censuring eyes of the boss.

A lot of people do a lot of rationalizing about thinking; one would guess that they fear it, and, in fact, it can be hard work. For example, I sat on a board of directors for several years in which there was much occupation with trivia and matters that should never have been bucked up to the board to begin with. In response to my criticism that we needed some planning time—some blue-sky time just to let our thoughts roam over the future—we arranged the schedule to do just that. But we always found other ways to fill it. The reluctance to be creative probably flows both from never having been trained to be so and from a fear of unstructured time and activity.

How did I achieve this free time? I learned about delegating. The first important thing is to know what you want when you assign a task to a subordinate. Some managers make vague assignments and say, "Don't worry, I know what I want, even if I can't express it. I'll know it when I see it." That robs the employee of a sense of achievement as well as self-confidence. The employee should be able to know the desired result of his or her effort in advance. If you can take the time to encourage the employee to shape the output at the time of assignment, you'll have a subordinate who feels a greater sense of ownership in the project. Greater ownership usually means greater commitment.

Almost as important as knowing what you want is finding out how the employee feels about the task you're delegating. This is a step that many managers bypass. They simply assume that the employee can do the job, largely because the manager can. The manager projects his or her ability onto the employee, who sits there feeling the confidence drain away. Not wishing to admit that he or she has reservations about the project, the employee leaves the manager's office with the boss believing that all is well. Later, mistakes or procrastination by the employee will show that, indeed, not all is well. It's necessary therefore to get a feel for how the employee looks at the job. Ask the subordinate how he or she plans to do it, whether the subordinate foresees problems, and what kind of schedule the subordinate believes is realistic. Ask. And listen. Watch for signs of uncertainty and hesitation. Be alert also to unrealistic expectations that may suggest the employee is compensating for his or her doubt. Don't let the employee leave your office without your having a sense of the self-confidence he or she is feeling about doing the task.

What's your role? You cannot abdicate your responsibility. Are you a resource? To what extent can the employee call on you if there is a difficulty? How will you maintain control? How often will you monitor or expect a progress report? These issues are best determined at the outset of the job, not later when the employee might believe that your controlling techniques indicate a lack of confidence in him or her. A controlling or monitoring contract that is agreed upon at the time of assignment and followed accordingly will usually not result in resentment.

When the employee has made satisfactory progress, you must compliment him or her. When the employee runs into trouble, you must take corrective action—as quickly as possible. The employee who does the job well needs reinforcement and encouragement. The employee who flounders needs to be put on the right path quickly; otherwise he or she will feel unmotivated and confused. And when the job is done to the standards that you and the employee discussed originally, you must find a way to recognize the achievement with some form of reward.

Unfortunately, in some cases, being lazy is a burden you inflict on others. It reminds me of the comment made by a contemporary of Saint John Stylites, who seldom took a bath: The odor of his sanctity became a cross for others to bear. As a lazy person, I don't like details. That's fine with a lot of subordinates who want their own chance to develop the means to get the job done. But occasionally I must collaborate with colleagues who want to be sure that every detail is thoroughly discussed in advance. My laziness and relative indifference to details become their cross. By shrugging my shoulders and giving my coworkers latitude, I think I am bestowing a compliment: I trust you and I know you'll do fine. But my colleagues may believe that I am simply indifferent.

Thus, I have to temper my laziness. When people display what I regard as a pathological attention to the inputs, I must be tolerant and be prepared to work with them because that's their value system. They are into activities.

The lazier I become, the more I enjoy the freedom that it brings me and the harder it is for me to collaborate. I have become a loner—but a loner who is dedicated to results.

And now you know my secret. This piece is not really about laziness at all, is it? It's about control. Paraphrasing the proverb, if you would be lazy, you must have control. And that, I'll bet, is a relationship you probably didn't think about much.

Chapter 5

Managing Your Time
Means Managing Your Life

I once wrote an article for a training magazine daring to confess that traditional time management programs don't work for me. If you've been in organizational life very long, you'll recognize them. They suggest that you prioritize your tasks and paper by categorizing them as A—most important, B—of average importance, C—probably not worth bothering about, or that you make time logs to evaluate the importance of what you do, or other similar structures. Generally speaking, traditional approaches emphasize imposing external discipline to help you get control of your life.

I think I also wrote that I didn't really believe such approaches helped most people because their proponents seem to assume that perceptions of time are rooted in the left brain. (Judging by the letters of protest the magazine received in response to my article, the time management constituency is quite vocal.) That is, all one needs to do to manage time is to be very rational and analytical. Ironically, one of the most logical and analytical people I ever knew was hopelessly lost in trying to control her time. She was as compulsively late as I am compulsively punctual—you could have given her all the letters in the alphabet to help her prioritize and they wouldn't have had any impact. Early on, I realized that it was I who would make compromises, not she. I would arrange to meet her somewhere with a bar because I knew that she might keep me waiting for thirty or forty-five minutes.

I confess that I don't know precisely where the time-controlling mechanism is in me, but I don't think it's entirely on the logical and analytical side of my brain. No, I suspect that one's perception of time and its value are all mixed up with the rational and the nonrational—intuition, emotions. And let's not forget cultural influences; in some parts of the world, an arrangement to meet someone on Wednesday might involve guessing which of the fifty-two is meant.

If my theory is correct—and now that I'm approaching sixty years of age you might be tempted to give it some credence—then the traditional approaches that emphasize logical procedures probably don't have a lasting effect on people who have been exposed to them. There is, of course, the high that people carry out of the training room based on the hope that, at long last, they are about to get their acts together. But following procedures and formulas can, in my experience, prove to be a bore.

Nevertheless, time management training is very popular. How can we explain that? For one thing, there is a very natural desire to be in control of something, especially in these turbulent times when you may suspect that most things are out of control and that you are powerless to do much about them. Along come nice people who show you how to impose external discipline to put you in control, again or for the first time.

My second explanation for the popularity of time management training is, I fear, a bit cynical. And it is that time management is a harmless idea. Top management and training directors can ordain such training without fear that any negative consequences will occur. And there is no unfavorable implication in conducting time management training, as there might be in scheduling communication training for people who don't talk to one another. In one company with which I was associated for a time, the management trainer, who was new to the organization, interviewed all of us managers prior to designing a three-day session. We told her that communication was nil—up, down, and sideways—that there was much distrust among the top, the middle, and the bottom, that morale was nonexistent, and that sound management practices were the exception rather than the rule. She listened politely, reported to her superiors, and delivered to us a time management program. It was the safest decision she could have made.

Philosophically, Alan Lakein, one of the pioneers of time management training, had it right when he presented his approach, in the lectures he gave and which I heard, as taking control "of your time and your life." The essence of controlling time is indeed the control of one's life. But imposing some external procedures and discipline in an attempt to reshape the inner person is, I believe, going about it in a backward manner. You must, I am convinced, proceed from the inner person out.

To manage time successfully, I propose, you must be achievement oriented rather than activities oriented. Measure your output rather than your input. We tend to be an input-centered society. People often find it hard to distinguish between their activities and what those activities are supposed to accomplish. Having a full calendar seems to give meaning to the day. Having a full agenda for a meeting indicates good planning. George Odiorne of Management by Objectives (MBO) fame called it, in a lecture I attended in 1967, the *activity trap*. It has always been a favorite phrase of his. In my field, trainers are very susceptible to overemphasizing inputs. Recently I heard a training director boast that, in her company, 400 people went through time management training in one year. She was elated. We trainers like to warm chairs. But what was the effect, I wondered? Did people now enjoy early dinners because they knew how to save 25 percent of their time? Better yet, did the company now enjoy 22 percent greater productivity from all the trainees? The results are seldom trumpeted. But the classrooms and the trainers were busy.

People who are skillful in controlling time measure their output rather than their input. They feel success not by how much they can cram into their schedules but by how much they can accomplish. The ends are what count. Everything else falls into place—a subordinate place. Time need not be the enemy, as people often express. Time need be only what you make it. It is, if nothing else, simply a medium.

I'll share with you what works well for me. It is probably far more intuitive and instinctive than rational.

Develop a Fairly Accurate Perception of the Passage of Time. Years ago I read the story of a clever trial attorney who, knowing that his witness would be asked to demonstrate her ability to estimate the time between certain events pertaining to the case, made her practice guessing the passage of time until she was practically on the second.

That's a good idea for anyone, without the pressure, of course. The next time you want to check your watch to see what time it is, guess first what time it might be. Then look at your watch. If you do this regularly, you'll eventually become rather accurate. Instead of the befuddled person who loses himself or herself in time, then looks at a clock and exclaims, "Good heavens, it's ten already," you can be the confident person who announces, "It must be about ten," and, checking, finds that it is ten minutes to. You can become so skilled that you'll almost never lose track of time, which is not, I warn you, an unmixed blessing.

Assign a Time Value to Each Task. The traditional time management approach, I suppose, would involve breaking the task down into segments and estimating a completion time for each one. Then you add them up. But that's quite time-consuming. I use a trial-and-error method until I get more precise. In fact, I borrowed it from the artillery. It involves bracketing. The artillery spotter, directing the fire of the guns behind him, estimates range to the target, initially excessively. The shells consequently fall beyond the target. Then the spotter estimates short. The shells fall short. Gradually, by decreasing the far estimate, and lengthening the short, the spotter guides the shells to the target. I estimate the time it will take me to do the task, conservatively at first, then overoptimistically, and I finally arrive at a fairly accurate time. I confess that I'm usually more conservative than not, and I have a certain amount of time left over to do things I hadn't known I could be doing in that time frame.

Once you become even proximately accurate in estimating the time value of tasks, you'll find that one significant benefit is that you don't allow yourself to become overcommitted. You'll carry around your schedule in your head. You'll accept projects and deadlines you're confident you can meet, and you can negotiate on those you suspect you can't. Another benefit is that people will love to deal with you, instead of with those bumbleheads who say that a job will be a piece of cake, a day or so at the maximum, and then, only after much prodding and swearing by others, finish it two weeks late. I saved for last the sweetest benefit of knowing how long it will take you to do tasks: You'll benefit from a vast reduction in anxiety. Life is a great deal more pleasant when you don't have to worry every day or every week about your ability to come through on time.

Limit Distractions. This is the point at which the discipline comes in. Or perhaps it's the motivation to achieve. Become ruthless about what you want to finish or what you believe is important to finish. A friend of mine could start four jobs in an hour, get a phone call about a fifth, start that, and perhaps never finish any of them. All her energy was dissipated among too many activities. But to the achiever, everything other than the priority task gets shoved aside, if possible. When I'm working on an important project such as a book, the first class mail requiring attention goes to my desk where I cannot miss it. The other letters, pamphlets, and brochures pile up on my coffee table—and even on my floor—until I'm done. It's called horizontal filing, I believe. If I don't achieve what I've set for myself on a given day, I send myself to bed early so that I can get up earlier the next day to make it up. No television tonight for you, buster.

Negotiate Deadlines. People frequently get into time squeezes when they automatically assume other people's deadlines, or what they assume those deadlines to be. My standard question is, "When do you have to have this?" I'm usually pleased to find that it isn't as soon as I had thought. An editor phoned me a couple of years back to tell me that he needed two articles as quickly as possible for a publication he was launching. Although I was busy, I heard the panic in his voice and wanted to help him out. I had visions of dropping everything to write two articles. As soon as possible turned out to be a comfortable two weeks—for the first article alone.

When people try to back you against the wall with deadlines that you feel are unreasonable, remember George S. Kaufman's question to MGM executive producer Irving Thalberg, who was pressuring him for a script. "Mr. Thalberg," Kaufman asked, "do you want it Wednesday, or do you want it good?"

Go with Your Energy Curves. There are times of the day—and night—when you feel more like working than at other times. At such times you have more energy, and you can accomplish much more than during other hours. As a manager of both morning people and afternoon people, I used to schedule meetings for the late morning. The morning folks were still at peak, and those who were slow risers were just beginning to wake up.

I have two peak times during the day. (At night, forget it.) My best period is between eight in the morning and noon. My energy curve goes up again at about three in the afternoon, but it's not as high as in the morning. Between noon and three, I do less demanding tasks such as reading, taking walks, napping, and talking on the phone. If I start a project on the energy upswing, I can accomplish two to three times what I can when the curve is low.

Be Good to Yourself. If you want to accomplish a great deal in a short time, or when you must work through depressions of the energy curve, divide the job into segments and find ways to reward yourself after finishing each. For example, when I'm doing a book, I'll set myself a subgoal of three pages before I can have a cup of coffee. Two more pages until I can check for the mail. I have to do four pages before I can read the *Wall Street Journal*. Three more, and lunch or a phone call to a friend. Work, reward, work, reward. At my best, using the reward system, I've been able to turn out twenty to twenty-five manuscript pages in a day. One note of caution: Martinis are not good as a reward during the day. True, you can get awfully happy about what you have accomplished, but at the same time you can get even happier about not doing any more.

There you have it: my secret of time management. It may not be popular with time management trainers, but generally speaking, it allows me to do all the things that I must and some of the things that time management experts say I shouldn't. For example, I remember Alan Lakein saying that I should never touch a particular piece of paper more than once. But listen, when you get a letter complimenting you on a speech or a review saying that your book is great, well, that's a piece of paper you'd like to handle more than once. Say, twenty or thirty times.

Part Two

CREATING A
PARTNERSHIP WITH
YOUR SUBORDINATES

*I*t has been almost thirty years since Douglas McGregor published his famous book *The Human Side of Enterprise* with its famous distinction between Theory X and Theory Y. Theory X, of course, is a traditional—as McGregor put it—assumption about people: They really don't want to work; they must be coerced and threatened in order to produce on the job. Theory Y is a more contemporary view of people: Work is important to employees.

The traditional perceptions are still with us. The manager must direct, control, monitor, and discipline. That's true. But what seems to be unconventional for many managers is the reality—I use the word confidently—that most employees want to work and to work well. The majority of us satisfy many of our goals through our work. Everything a manager can do to help employees achieve their own goals through helping the manager to gain his or hers is motivational.

In fact, managers and employees should seek contracts with one another. If I do a good job for you, the employee offers, you, the manager, will reward me for my effort. You will help me to get what I want. The concept of a contract between employer and employee is clearly a Theory Y perspective. And Theory Y is by no means as widely accepted as we'd like to believe it is.

There's an added urgency these days in the increased global competition and the excellent performance of our competitors in Asia and Europe. We in this country often find ourselves undersold and outproduced. The contract of which I speak should be based solely on performance, not on longevity, personality, or congeniality. What I want from you is good performance, the manager insists. All rewards will be based on that.

But there has been a danger in many people's interpretation of Theory Y. All people are not alike. There are people who justify Theory X assumptions—people who must be closely directed, controlled, monitored, and disciplined. Thus, there is no one way to manage. Even though the correct trend is toward a participative, democratic workplace, there is room for other styles of managing. There are, for example, times when an autocratic style is quite appropriate and effective.

All of the above seem to justify the ultimate ambiguous statement, left over from college philosophy: All generalizations are false including this one. When I use it in speeches, it usually gets a laugh, but it's a laugh of recognition.

Partners make contracts, and that's what this section is about: partnership.

Chapter 6

Looking Beyond the Person to the Behavior

Could there possibly be anyone in America who doesn't remember the scene in *The Wizard of Oz* in which kindly old Frank Morgan, who plays the wizard, is unmasked as a fake? Dorothy and her three friends are standing in awe in the wizard's chamber listening to his booming voice and seeing the fearful face on the screen above them when her dog, Toto, runs over to a curtained booth and pulls the curtain aside to reveal Morgan working levers and speaking into a microphone. Dorothy, incensed at the deception, accuses the would-be wizard of being a bad man. He replies, "I'm not a bad man; I'm just a bad wizard."

That quotation, framed, would be a useful addition to any manager's wall because it's a reminder that what people do is separate from who they are. In managing, we deal with what people do, not with what they are. Or at least we should relate to people that way. Unfortunately, we managers often characterize people by traits and personality rather than by behavior. Centuries ago, the church developed its advice: Love the sinner; hate the sin. Unfortunately, managers do often feel sinned against by others, and it's probably not useful to reinforce the perception that there are sinners out there sinning against us. There's quite enough vindictiveness already in our organizations.

I've always felt that transactional analysis (TA) conveys one of the healthiest messages a manager can receive: I'm OK; you're OK. A lot of managers don't think that some people they work with are OK; they see them as sinners or adversaries who may be out to get them. The employee who doesn't seem motivated to do a good job is lazy. The manager who disagrees is playing politics and wants to win "at my expense." The boss with whom one does not get along well plays favorites and is unfair.

We personalize our disagreement. We go after the person rather than the behavior or issue. For example, a woman reported to me that she had a problem with her counterpart in another department. She had wanted to consult with him on a project she was in charge of, and he had agreed. She sent him some important documents that he was to review from the perspective of his expertise. She didn't hear back from him by the deadline she had imposed, so she called his office. (She couldn't make a visit to him because he was located at some distance.) He didn't return the call. She called again and again and again. No response. Angry and desperate, she wrote him a letter, with a copy to me. She described his failure to respond to her phone calls and then said, "Your behavior simply is not professional. I guess you don't want this project to succeed."

I criticized her letter. She had, I said, committed two sins. She had labeled his behavior (not professional) and had suggested an uncomplimentary motive (not wanting this project to succeed). She responded with, "All I did was to describe what he did." "No, you didn't," I answered. Once again, I told her about her labeling and characterizing, but to no avail. She was totally convinced that she had done nothing more than describe his behavior.

The question of whether he deserved the label is not the point here. When dealing with others, the only aspect of those people we are truly competent to deal with is their behavior. You can see it. You can hear it. You can describe it. You are an expert in your perceptions. That doesn't mean that another person is going to agree with all of your perceptions. Remember the famous Japanese movie *Rashomon,* which describes the differing perceptions of people who were involved in or witnessed a crime? The other person cannot deny that you had such perceptions. He or she can only say, "That's not what I saw." Not—and this is crucial—"It didn't happen that way." While there may be occasional disagreements about what was seen or heard, there's often some common ground that people can come to terms on.

But when you enter the world of attitudes and motives, it is murky indeed. After you express yourself strongly in a meeting, what happens when someone asks you, "Why are you so angry?" If you weren't angry before, you probably are following that question. Or, in the same meeting, when you respond intently to someone's disagreement with an idea you have presented, and another says, "There's no need to get defensive," you get defensive. People are analyzing you and labeling you. Perhaps you didn't see yourself as angry or defensive. If not, chances are you'll argue that you were not. Meanwhile the main issue is lost. And even if you were angry or defensive, so what? Remember that analyzing or labeling is one way to deflect you from the issue and, at least for the moment, to render you less effective.

When someone believes that he or she can intrude on my person with impunity, that person makes me feel vulnerable. At the least I feel open to harm and at the most I feel violated. Ironically, the other might have had honorable intentions of telling me something about myself that I ought to know. I can recall an incident years ago about which I still feel a residue of irritation. Shortly before, I had taken over the editorship of a weekly publication, an experience quite new to me. Between the staff we had and some freelance writers, I was receiving ample copy to fill each issue. I was concentrating on editing and doing little or no writing. My boss called me into her office and, hesitantly, lectured me on my lack of growth since I had taken over the publication. It was for me—and for her, I suspect—a difficult interview. The message I heard was, "Now that you've got this good job, I won't let you coast." In TA terms it was: I'm OK; you're not OK.

Today, I would counsel her to give me the feedback in a different way. For example, "I see that you are not writing regularly as you used to do, and I'm sorry about that, for you as well as for us. You have ideas to contribute, and we're not getting the benefit of them. You, I think, get your sense of achievement and growth through your writing. Writing, I suspect, helps you think, as it does me. At any rate, I'd like to see you contribute at least an article every other week."

Everything she said during the real interview was true, but I felt bad because I felt as if I were lacking in some important way—as if I had been accused of being smug, lazy, and content to coast. It would indeed have been much more useful to me and less hurtful if she had simply pointed out that both the company and I needed me to write regularly.

It is this unnecessary and unwarranted invasion of the person that causes so many employees to dread performance appraisals. The object of an appraisal should be to help the employee to be more effective. Instead, many evaluations ask the appraiser to pass judgment on matters that have little to do with performance—matters such as personality characteristics including maturity or enthusiasm, or inputs such as loyalty, initiative, or working well with others. The proper emphasis is on what the employee does that is useful to the organization—the results rather than the activity. If, during the appraisal period, the employee performs unsuccessfully, there should be, in connection with the evaluation, an action plan for improvement. To describe someone as congenial, cooperative, or willing to take on responsibility tells the reader very little about a person's ability to achieve agreed-upon organizational goals.

Employees usually have no objection to performance appraisals and interviews that are designed and conducted to make them more effective. In fact, far from having objections, most employees welcome a review and evaluation of their accomplishments. However, they do (correctly, I think) resent evaluations that require the subjective measurement by a boss or evaluations that focus on attitudes and motives that can't be seen or measured at all. The only thing that can be measured is behavior, and that should be evaluated in terms of goals accomplished rather than in terms of investment of time and energy. In short, as an employee, I may have been unsuccessful in some of my projects or goals, but by no means should an evaluation suggest that I am an unsuccessful person.

Having become almost fanatic in preaching that there is a difference between judging a person by who he or she is and by what he or she does or can do, I'm beginning to appreciate at least some of the meaning behind Will Rogers's mystifying comment, "I never met a man I didn't like." To say that, you have to be able to see the person apart from what the person may do. (It revolts me to say this, but many people found Hitler charming and quite likable when he wasn't murdering people.) I can't say that I'm totally in harmony with Rogers's consummate good will, but as I grow older, I do find that I have a lot more tolerance for people—even though I may not like some of their behaviors. In various activities I've found colleagues maddening in their compulsion to pick nits, boring in their long-windedness, shallow in their analyses, reprehensible in their desires to avoid signficant issues, and unpleasant in their hostility (sometimes toward me). But I seldom have turned down invitations to drink with them after work. I may not have liked working with them, but I saw them as nice, congenial, interesting human beings. I didn't mind socializing with them; I just didn't always like to work with them.

If you study Will Rogers's humor, you will notice that he did not attack persons. He made fun of their behavior, and sometimes he did it in such a charming way that his target enjoyed it most. There's a famous newsreel of Rogers roasting Franklin D. Roosevelt in Los Angeles after the 1932 presidential campaign. The president-elect is shown standing a few feet away, frequently throwing his head back in laughter at Rogers's sallies. The humorist was not malicious, although foibles were legitimate targets. Coming back from a trip to Egypt in the 1920s, he told reporters about the sights, although he said he hadn't seen the sphinx; he had already seen Mr. Coolidge.

Rogers provides a model for all of us. Criticize people's behavior. Dislike it, if you will. Poke a little fun at it. But respect the person behind it. I'm OK; you're OK. But let's talk about your behavior that I don't like. Organizations would be friendlier to work in if those who are in them observed the distinction.

Frank Morgan was right. Do you honestly think that Frank Morgan could ever have played a bad man? Not on your life.

Chapter 7

Motivation Is the Book, Not the Chapter

*A*kin to the spirit of the famous comment about the weather (which, I'm told, Mark Twain did *not* make), everyone talks about motivation, but it's rather difficult to see what anyone is doing about it. A publisher once told me that if I wanted to see my book on employee motivation just sit on a bookstore shelf, I should put the word motivation in the title. I decided to prove him wrong. Fearlessly, I included the M word in my title—and proved him right.

But if you talk to the average CEO about the importance of having a motivated work force, you'll hear, "Oh, absolutely. That's our top priority." Motivated people are committed people, and when they commit themselves to the achievement of organizational goals, they produce more and better. "Unquestionably," says the CEO. So the subject of employee motivation should occupy a prominent place in your management training programs. "We agree wholeheartedly," the CEO concurs.

He or she may agree, but motivation usually isn't prominent. Prominent often means that motivation is one module out of twelve. Or it might be a subset of another module, say, leadership skills. If it's Tuesday morning, it must be motivation. And what is taught may be so generic as to defy application, such as the theory that a professor at the University of Michigan proudly explained to me as his own development. I asked, "Well, what does a manager do with it?" He seemed astonished that I would ask. "I don't know," he said. Other theories of motivation are specific and complicated, such as Maslow's hierarchy, or ambiguous, as is Herzberg's.

The result for managers is a mixed message that says you should know how people are motivated, but it's really not important enough for us to figure out how you can put this knowledge to use. In fact, many managers, even after training, continue to believe that motivation is something you *do* to someone. Frederick Herzberg's acronym KITA describes this attitude well: kick in the ass. Or perhaps more humanely, you add a carrot now and then. I once knew a corporate treasurer who told his people, "If you do good work, I'll let you keep your job." He was only half kidding.

Management is usually presented in bits and pieces. Motivation is only a subset without a context. Trainees may see management, unfortunately, as a series of discrete acts that may have little or nothing to do with one another. We throw what I call skills packages at managers—a day of delegation, two days of interpersonal relations, a half day of communication, an hour or two of how to appraise, and so on. Management development begins to resemble a jigsaw puzzle, and, back on the job, few managers find the time to put it all together. As before the training session the manager fails to ask, when communicating to employees or giving assignments, what the impact will be on their motivation.

The retention curve is our enemy. Without rewards for application, the new knowledge remains in the head for a short time. Without application, there is little real learning.

One answer to the relative failure of many management development programs is to provide trainees with a context, an umbrella, a system. What is the one factor that is present in every action that a manager takes with subordinates? It is the impact on employees' motivation. Everything a manager does in directing or coordinating the work of employees has some effect on their motivation and commitment to work effectively. Thus, the management of employees' motivation should be the determining consideration behind how managers behave toward their subordinates—how they communicate, how they assign, how they reward, how they develop. Therefore, the presentation of skills for managing people should be in the context of how application of those skills will increase the motivation, the commitment, and the effectiveness of those people.

To be credible, any discussion of motivation must be firmly rooted in a simple, universal, easily translated theory base. As readers of my books and articles know, my base has always been

Expectancy Theory. It's simple, and it has been around for a long time. It's mainstream psychology. And it works. Expectancy Theory explains that human behavior is a function of (1) the perceived value of the reward that will follow certain behavior and (2) the expectation in the doer's mind that he or she can actually enjoy such a reward. In choosing among courses A, B, and C, whether the decision involves a career, a job, an activity for the morning, or what one will have for lunch, a person will select the option that results in the biggest reward, so long as he or she believes the reward is available without taking undue risk. Long shots don't motivate most people—except gamblers, perhaps.

Thus, people always act for reasons of their own, and those reasons have to do with rewards—money, pleasure, taste, satisfaction, and so on. What's the application of the theory? Managers have the power to increase the value of the work and the power to increase the attainability of the valued reward. And managers can take five steps to accomplish both ends. (1) Tell employees what you expect them to do, (2) make the work valuable, (3) make the work doable, (4) while employees are trying to do what you expect, give them feedback, and (5) when employees have done what you expected, reward them.

Not only do these five steps constitute an overview of motivation, they also create the context in which management development programs should be designed. Instead of presenting skills separately, we should shape them to enable managers to know how to effect each of the five steps. Such a design would turn most management training and development approaches over on their heads. Let's take a look at each step in detail.

Tell Employees What You Expect Them to Do. Probably one of the more common reasons for the failure of many Management by Objectives attempts is that most managers don't believe they have to sit down periodically with employees and talk about their goals and standards of performance. They just don't think they have to. "Why, my employees already know what I want—or should." In many cases, the employees think they do know what the boss wants, but the result is often what the boss doesn't want.

The first task in a management development course is to show managers that they must communicate their goals and standards to subordinates on a regular basis, instead of simply assuming that employees know what the managers want and can read their managers' minds: "Don't worry, I'll know it when I see it." When the goal isn't even a figment of the manager's imagination, the employee hardly knows where to begin or how to proceed.

A second task is to train managers in interviewing skills so that they learn not only how to communicate their wishes but also how to make sure the employees understand what they hear. I would add some training in negotiating skills at this stage, because the more the employee has a say in the goals that are established, the more he or she, in today's psychological jargon, owns those goals—the more important they are to the employee. Furthermore, if the employee helps to shape the goals, then undoubtedly he or she is doing so with personal objectives in mind. In short, the employee is thinking, "I will help you to achieve these goals because doing so will help me reach my own," which might be achievement, higher status, advancement, growth and development, money, and so on.

Listening is a very relevant skill at this stage—to sense whether the employee understands what the manager is asking and to assess the degree of commitment.

If the manager is fortunate enough to have an appraisal system that is tied to goals and performance, he or she will find this stage much more relevant and acceptable to employees than it would otherwise be. What a relief it must be for employees to say to themselves, "I'm going to be evaluated strictly on how well I perform, not on whether I'm mature, enthusiastic, or loyal and not on whether I show initiative, or work well with others. All that counts is what I do in achieving the goals we've set." Most appraisal programs I've encountered are silly and irrelevant. They concern themselves with inputs when what really matters is output. They ask managers to judge employees' motives and attitudes, which can't be seen or measured. Such appraisals are not only worthless but often humiliating and punitive.

Make the Work Valuable. At this stage of a manager's activity, things get a bit complicated. The manager who has thirty subordinates may have thirty sets of motivating factors. Management principles, I always say, are few and simple. They apply to everyone. But management practice is complicated; it's one-to-one.

Managers need to know about the power of employees' internal rewards—the ones employees give themselves. Some people are turned on by achieving or being competitive—achieving more than others. Others are crafts oriented; they like being good at certain kinds of work. Many employees are looking for more satisfaction, advancement, or self-esteem. Where possible, managers should provide the kind of work that will help employees attain these rewards.

Unfortunately, many managers project their values onto employees. They seem to say, this is what I like and this is what you employees should like. For example, a friend of mine once lost his job when, after three years of doing the same tasks, he confessed to his boss that he was bored. His boss had been doing essentially the same work for twenty years and was quite content. My friend's restlessness outraged him.

When training managers, we need to show them how to collect and to interpret personal data about employees that will help them understand who will be gratified by what kind of work. Here is another stage at which interviewing skills are important, in order to avoid threatening employees by seeming to pry into their personal interests. Of course, if the appraisal program is built on performance and accomplishment, the manager has a rich source of data.

The manager can also add value to the work by providing external rewards for work well done. In workshops, I often tell managers to forget about money as a reward. Their companies give too little of it too late. A pay increase that everyone gets in January doesn't relate to much that may have gone on the previous spring. An enterprising manager, with the help of a trainer, can come up with twelve, fifteen, maybe even twenty or more ways to say thank you. Look for perks and privileges—more control over one's work, more responsibility, more challenge, new furniture or equipment, a dinner on the boss, or training for advanced skills. I once had supervisors in one organization tell me they'd love to see doors on their cubicles. I told them, "Perform well, and you get a door." The essential message managers need to convey is, "Around here, when you do a good job, you'll be recognized for it."

Interviewing skills would be a helpful tool when training managers to evaluate the worth of the task to an employee. And in actually adding value to the work, a short workshop on delegation would be relevant.

Make the Work Doable. Managers could benefit from training in giving assignments. They often think the process is simple when in fact it is complex. Often they are not clear and specific about what they want done; they don't satisfy themselves that the employees have understood the assignment (another case of managers' projecting their own understandings and abilities onto employees); they don't establish a monitoring contract (how often and how they will check up). Sometimes, when managers choose the wrong person to do a task, the work is doomed from the start.

Interviewing skills are a must. Managers need to find out what is on the employees' minds. In many instances, employees sit there and nod, whether they understand what the manager wants or not. Then they go out and try to do it, and when they botch it, the manager thinks they don't care or are rebellious. Or because they don't think they can do it, the employees become unmotivated, in which case, the manager asks, "What can you do with employees who have lost the work ethic?"

Once the manager determines that an employee is uncertain about how to do a task or is unsure of his or her ability to do it, the manager must be prepared to train or to coach, each of which is a training module. Adults learn differently from children, a distinction that some trainers seem to be unaware of. Children learn because they know if they don't they won't get out of school. Adults need specific reasons to learn. You must show them why it is in their interests to learn. While they learn, you must give them feedback. And you must provide opportunities for application of what they are learning. When the application has been successful, employees need to be reinforced and rewarded.

Coaching takes patience and skill. The manager must know how to coach the employee through a problem or obstacle without providing all of the solution and without demanding that the employee assume all the burden for coming up with the answer. Many employees are quite adept at reverse delegation—letting their managers do their work for them. And many managers are unaware of the motivating possibilities in a good coaching session. When an employee has, even with the manager's help, worked through a problem to a solution, the sense of satisfaction, perhaps even excitement, fires up the motivating forces.

While Employees Are Trying to Do What You Expect, Give Them Feedback. This stage demands several modules: interviewing, on-the-spot feedback techniques, counseling, and coaching, to begin with. My experience in conducting workshops through the years leads me to believe that most managers feel no great confidence in giving feedback, and they often give it in such a way that the employees become unmotivated. It's vital that managers see feedback as an essential part of managing the motivation of employees. Feedback is never received neutrally by employees. It either helps or it doesn't. And if it doesn't help, it may hurt.

A basic problem with managers and their feedback is that they want to be liked. They don't want to cause pain, for themselves or for employees—unless of course the problems continue, in which case the managers may get angry and blow up, usually succeeding in making everything worse. There may indeed be some pain in insisting on correction, but most employees will endure it. They don't want to be ineffective, so the sooner the manager takes corrective action, the better.

I don't agree with those who say that you should combine negative with positive. They say that the manager should find something good about the employee to ease the pain and to help restore the employee's self-esteem. Combining positive and negative creates misunderstandings, especially if it leads the manager to employ the sandwich technique, which I describe as a slab of criticism between two thin slices of praise. The praise dilutes the criticism, and the criticism contaminates the praise.

Managers should be trained to keep the message clean. If you want to correct a problem, fine. If you want to reinforce someone positively, do that. But if possible, do them separately. There should be no mixed messages for employees.

Coaching for growth and development is a feedback function that managers usually don't perform, especially if they're busy putting out fires. But when a manager sits down with an employee and reviews that employee's strengths and potential in the light of the employee's career plans, the manager gives perhaps the most powerful feedback of all. And the employee will probably regard the session as a reward—recognition of work well done.

With growing frequency, one sees training modules that help the manager deal with problem employees. Some corrective action is successful when criticism is given promptly (while employees can still remember doing what the manager is upset about), but in the more resistant cases, counseling is indicated. And woe to the manager and to the company if counseling is not provided before termination or discipline. These days the door is wide open to a law suit. Counseling requires special interviewing techniques, and it's safe to say that most managers don't possess them.

As for appraising, I have other biases in addition to my belief that the only worthwhile evaluation is one that accurately represents performance levels—quantity and quality. And one is that there should be no surprises for employees when it comes to appraisals. Because performance is tied to goals, employees should know in advance what managers will say. Another is my belief that many trainers are training managers how to use appraisal systems that the trainers know won't work properly, however much training goes on.

When Employees Have Done What You Expected, Reward Them. In survey after survey, employees confirm the awful truth: They do not see the rewards they get as tied to their performance. One such study, conducted a few years ago by the Public Agenda Foundation of New York, revealed that 78 percent of employees contacted did not believe there was a direct relationship between how hard they worked and how much they were paid.

Managers could use an intense workshop in the Skinnerian principles of behavior conditioning or modification. Chances are that most managers are not systematically and effectively using rewards they have at their disposal to shape the behavior they want in employees. Most managers are too often lax in giving praise and other forms of positive reinforcement because they don't understand intermittent maintenance of the behavior already shaped.

The guiding principle behind any reward is this: Reward the behavior you want; don't reward the behavior you don't want. And I'll add the following to that: Don't reward on the basis of anything that doesn't contribute to your getting the performance you want from your subordinates.

I suppose that at this point some might say I now have the tail wagging the dog. In fact, we do treat motivation as an appendage, like a tail, instead of treating it as a brain—the controlling element. All of the training modules I've mentioned have their place in helping managers to manage the motivation of subordinates—the most important job managers have. These modules should be presented in that context. When people are presented with a system that has an inner logic, they learn faster and they remember it longer.

When it comes to training managers in the facts of motivation, we're doing things backward when we offer the subject as a subset—a rather theoretical and not very pertinent module. Presented that way, it doesn't seem to be very important knowledge for managers. If they treat it as unimportant, they won't apply it, and motivation will continue to be the neglected subject it is. We'll continue to pay lip service—and a heavy price in lack of motivation.

Chapter 8

Negotiating Your Way
to Better Management

*L*ately I've begun to use a phrase that often causes
eyebrows to be raised: management by negotiation. The connotation departs from the traditional view of the manager who controls
and directs the work of subordinates. The smart manager, however,
realizes that employees are partners in the operation. They bring
skills, experience, knowledge, and other resources to the job. But,
say some managers, if I treat employees as partners, what about our
prerogatives as managers?

I don't give much credence to managerial prerogatives,
probably because I suspect managers don't have as many as they
think they have. Today's work force is very capable, intelligent, and
enlightened, and I can hear them saying to their bosses, "Look, if
you want to think you're powerful, go right ahead. We'll let you
think that. If we like you, we'll even encourage you to think that
way. Just don't get in our way while we try to get the work done."
And the effective manager won't put obstacles in the way of
employees' effectiveness.

I think that the issue of managerial intelligence in negotiating takes precedence over the issue of prerogatives. Not only does
the smart manager not get in the way, he or she is likely to realize
that, if others have what the manager wants and needs, and if they
are not likely to give it up simply because the manager demands it,
negotiating skills can be very useful.

Incidentally, the words *needs* and *wants* are important in my
vocabulary because I'm a product of assertiveness training, which
got me started on this whole idea of managing by negotiation. The
purpose of assertiveness training is to help people identify their

needs and wants and to express those needs and wants in a manner acceptable to others. Thus, it's a valuable tool for communicating.

Assertiveness training, if I'm not mistaken, was a creation of the 1970s, concomitant with the rise of feminism. It was felt that women, presumably long confined to *kinder, küche,* and *kirche* (children, kitchen, and church), could benefit from learning how to assert themselves in the male-dominated world of business. On reflection, I don't see why women needed this more than men, but certainly, women at the time were more receptive to the notion. Having identified this kind of training with women, I was surprised one day to receive an announcement that the American Management Association was conducting assertiveness seminars for managers. It was a new wrinkle, I thought, so I looked into it.

The three-day program was the brainchild of Malcolm Shaw, a Connecticut consultant who believed that assertiveness should be more than simply a communicating tool. He properly positioned assertiveness on the spectrum of human behavior between aggressiveness, which is rolling over the rights and dignity of others, and nonassertiveness, which is rolling over and playing dead. (I want to digress for a moment to say that Shaw's seminar provided a good example of why training is sometimes viewed as a corrective process for deficiencies instead of as a growth experience. During the first hour, we all introduced ourselves and told the group why we were there. Roughly half of the participants said their bosses had sent them because they were too aggressive, while the other half told us their bosses regarded them as nonassertive. Transactional Analysis would have suggested that their bosses had conveyed the message I'm OK; you're not OK. They were expected to accept that discounting and change their behaviors in three days.)

I soon saw the rationale for Shaw's presenting assertiveness for managers. As I've already mentioned, he saw it as more than a tool for communicating and had added another mode of behavior to expand its usefulness: responsiveness. Basically, assertiveness gives me the vehicle for expressing what I want and need, and responsiveness does the same for you. The minute I assume that you are a partner in what is going on between us, it becomes a transaction. When I am responsive to you, I am acknowledging that you bring certain perceptions, strengths, resources, and agendas to the transaction. It's no longer simply a matter of my asserting myself to get what I want; I now grant that you may have something to contribute and to gain.

According to Shaw, there are four steps in the assertiveness mode of behavior: (1) a description of what I (the manager) see going on; (2) a description of how I feel about what is going on; (3) the change in you (the employee) that I want; and (4) the benefits to you resulting from the change.

For example, you are a manager who is upset with one of your employees because he has missed the deadlines on the last three projects you have given him. You call him into your office for a reprimand. Using the four steps of the assertiveness mode, here's how you might conduct the interview: (1) "John, I want to talk with you about the fact that you have turned in each of the last three projects after the deadline we agreed on." (2) "I'm very disappointed and upset. Also, I'm embarrassed because what I sent on to my boss was consequently late." (3) "In the future, I want you to respect the deadlines we set." (4) "When you do, I'll be able to give you better evaluations, and I'll feel comfortable letting you take on more important projects."

That's a perfectly clear-cut, straightforward bit of feedback. And indeed, many managers would feel that this is the end of the story. But if you suspect that your perceptions are not the whole story, you might choose to be responsive as well as assertive. The interview would go slightly differently because you would also observe the four steps of the responsive mode: (1) a description of what the employee probably sees going on; (2) a description of the employee's feelings about what is going on; (3) a desired change in you; and (4) the benefits to you resulting from the change.

Opening yourself up like that takes courage, but there could be some benefits that offset the risk. To illustrate, here's how the interview might go:

(1) "John, I want to talk with you about the fact that you have turned in each of the last three projects after the deadline we agreed on. Would you agree that that is an accurate assessment of the problem?"

The assertive-responsive mode has guided you to take an important step that many managers ignore in a feedback situation:

getting agreement from the employee that a problem exists. If the employee doesn't agree on the existence of the problem or on your perception of it, then there is little gain to be had by your plunging ahead with feedback.

John, however, agrees that your perception of the situation is correct.

(2) "I'm very disappointed and upset. Also, I'm embarrassed because what I sent on to my boss was consequently late. I would guess that you're not too happy about what has happened. Am I right?"

To your surprise, John responds, "I'm not only unhappy, I'm very angry about it." You ask why. "Well," John says, "I told you each time I took on a project that I might need to consult with you from time to time. There were some data involved I didn't have, and I didn't know where else to get them. You agreed to make yourself available. But every time I tried to see you, you'd put me off. Yes, I was late, because I had to get what I needed from other places, and that took time."

(3) "You're saying, John, that I'm part of the reason you were late and that in the future I should be more accessible to you."

John answers, "When we've agreed to that, yes."

(4) "Okay, and if I am reasonably accessible to you, you will make every effort to finish the work on time."

John's response: "Absolutely." John and you now have a contract, which you can remind him of when he takes another assignment from you. The results are much better than if you had simply asserted your wants and demanded that in the future John give them to you. John might have remained silent in his anger and walked out of the office a very resentful employee.

Conflict in organizations often has an adversarial, even paranoid, tone: "They refuse to cooperate." "They're just trying to wreck my project." "They're playing games with me." And when these attitudes dictate behavior of the disputants, managing conflict becomes largely an issue of preventing it from going completely out of control and causing great damage.

When managers use the assertive-responsive approach, they are often successful in reducing and even resolving the conflict. One advantage is the tone that is set; the people in conflict are each looking for a solution. Unfortunately, in much organizational conflict, the dispute gets personal, largely because one side or the other or both have decided that they are adversaries. Once that notion has taken hold, the respective stands become polarized. Since people who are polarized usually don't listen to each other (they are too busy trying to score points), the main issues become lost, and new issues are formed to keep the fire smoldering.

Without a formula such as the one assertiveness-responsiveness provides, it's very difficult for people on one side of the dispute to believe that those on the other side also want a solution. Much time and energy are often spent in establishing who was responsible for the problem to begin with. It's the phase variously described as "Who dunnit versus what do we do about it?" or, recalling the children's party game, "Whose donkey do we pin this tail on?" People in conflict can spend hours and hours pointing fingers at one another, thus diminishing any chance that, after the recriminations, anyone will want to work with the others in finding a solution or a way out of the morass.

From the outset, the manager, following the assertive-responsive formula, must acknowledge that the people on the other side have their own perceptions, which are probably as valid to them as the manager's are to him or her. And there is always the possibility that the other disputants are unhappy about the conflict and would like to work toward a solution that is acceptable to both sides. No doubt, the others also bring resources to the solution-finding effort.

As a consultant, I can testify that I've performed small miracles when I've been successful in getting people off the past, off the roots of the problem, off who was responsible, and onto doing something about it. One of the pioneers in group problem solving, Robert B. Morton, used to say to the groups he worked with, "If you don't like the situation that exists now, get together and define the alternative you can all accept." Anyone in organizational life can describe conflicts that have gone on so long that no one can quite remember how they started.

The assertive-responsive mode also imposes a discipline on the people who use it—a discipline they are frequently without: emphasis on behavior. Many misunderstandings and much resentment could be avoided if people, when giving feedback, confined their comments to descriptions of what they see and hear. Doing so doesn't necessarily result in absolute objectivity, but it lessens the chance that the problem will expand to issues that don't belong in it. For example, a manager says to an employee, "You have a poor work attitude." What does that mean? The employee feels put down and argues the point or goes away muttering. Unfortunately, that kind of dumb comment sometimes finds its way to the appraisal form, where it has no place. When giving feedback or trying to resolve a conflict, there's simply no place to talk about attitudes or motives. They can't be seen or measured, and often, they can't be agreed to. They divert energies that should be invested in solving the problem.

I'm sorry that assertiveness training has peaked. Relatively few people take it these days. It's one of the most valuable tools available, since, at one time or another, we all look for ways to frame unpleasant truths or thoughts in ways that won't get us punched in the nose. If people are to work together effectively, they have to say things that they'd rather not say. And they have to persuade people to listen to what they'd rather not hear.

And when people want something from others, they have to be prepared to negotiate for that need or want. Do you have a boss who bypasses you to give orders to your subordinates? Well, persuade that boss that you simply cannot be as effective for him or her as you'd like if the practice continues. Do you have a colleague who spreads untrue gossip about you? Well, convince the bum that it keeps the two of you from being able to work together to get the results you both want.

I think we're naive these days if we believe that we have a right to get what we want simply because we want or need it. That's an outmoded managerial perspective. We're more likely to get what we want by persuading others that it is in their interests to give us what we want. That's negotiating. And people who are successful in getting results they want in organizations tend to be people who manage that way. The familiar and traditional boss-subordinate relationship is being reshaped more as a partnership. And partners negotiate.

Chapter 9

Playing Favorites
Is Only Managing Fairly

*T*here's a telling line in Gilbert and Sullivan's *The Gondoliers:* "When everyone is somebody, then no one's anybody." The two gondoliers, one of whom might be a king (they don't, at this point, know which), have discovered aristocracy and forsworn republicanism. Perhaps, even in this era of the increasingly democratic workplace, managers need to do the same.

It's a point the U.S. Army might have recalled after the invasion of Grenada. Almost everyone got a medal. In fact, the total number of medals awarded was greater than the number of soldiers who participated. Somehow, as the gondoliers noted, when everyone gets a medal, it reduces the value of each one.

I sometimes startle managers when I tell them that, when it comes to awards and rewards, I am not a republican (with a small *r*). I have discovered elitism—an aristocracy: people who perform well. In an age in which we lament the downward slide of productivity and profess the need to compete with the output of other countries, we're awfully blasé and indiscriminate about our rewards to employees. The point is that if you want increased commitment and productivity from employees, that and that alone is what you reward them for. Otherwise your subordinates won't be sure of what they should do to get your recognition.

Listen to the following managers as they decide who merits raises.

"I'll bet Henry hasn't missed a day of work in thirty years. Anyone who is that conscientious deserves something."

"One thing about Andy: He never causes me any problems. No matter what I say, his response is always a cheerful, 'Okay boss.'"

"I always know what to expect of Sheila. Now, she may not be the best worker I have, but she's constant."

"Can you imagine? Harvey's in his forty-first year with the company. Guess we ought to commemorate that."

So management passes out watches and luggage and money and cameras, all in reward of what exactly? Henry and Harvey have occupied desks for many years, but there seems to be no consideration of how well they have performed at those desks. Andy doesn't rock the boat; in fact, he's quite docile and nonassertive—not really admirable qualities if you want a vibrant, high-output operation. And Sheila is constant. She probably has worked the same way for years, although undoubtedly the demands in the department have increased manifold.

What's the message that other employees receive? Hang on. Show up. Don't make waves. And don't kill yourself. Some priorities.

Priorities often get skewed in organizational life. A few years ago, a young supervisor took over the shipping department in a medium-size manufacturing company. Not long after, he entered into what we call an implicit bargain with his subordinates, who, for the most part, had been there longer and were older. The deal was this: If the supervisor didn't insist that when the end-of-break bell rang they immediately return to work, they would work harder. He didn't and they did. They began to ship 20 percent more than before. One day the young supervisor's boss passed through the shipping department a couple of minutes after the break had ended and saw the men still sitting around and talking. Furious, he called the young man into his office and gave him a tongue-lashing. Futilely, the supervisor explained that he was a bit easier on the men and that they worked harder for him. The boss demanded strict adherence to the rules. From that point on the men obeyed the bell and production returned to its previous level. Message: Around here, you are rewarded for following the rules—strictly.

In motivation, we preach that people have reasons for what they do—a revelation that often surprises managers who find that some of their employees indulge in mystifying behavior. Further, the reasons behind people's behaviors are always seen as good reasons to the doers—another fact that puzzles managers who see certain employees indulging in what the managers term self-destructive behavior. In short, people do only what they feel rewarded for doing.

If that is true, managers will ask, how do you get employees to change behavior that is not very productive or even counterproductive? Answer: Change the rewards. They're getting gratification for what they do now, so find a different and more appealing reward.

No, it isn't always as easy as it sounds. But if you don't change the reward, you're unlikely to alter the behavior you find objectionable. The late Herb Shepard, a very fine consultant, once told me about a case he had been called in on. Top management had instituted a weekly reporting system for supervisors. It had seemed simple and clear enough to top management, but the supervisors were either not doing it right or not doing it at all. Someone at the top suggested that perhaps the supervisors didn't fully understand why the reporting system was needed. The supervisors were oriented accordingly. Still top management failed to get the desired results. "Well," suggested another executive, "perhaps we ought to train them in how to do it. They understand why, but perhaps they don't know how." (You'll frequently notice that management will prescribe training when they don't know what else to do.) The reporting continued with only spotty success. Finally, after resorting to threats and getting poor results, top management called in Herb.

Good consultant that he was, Herb interviewed, surveyed, and eventually came up with the solution to the mystery. The reward that the supervisors were working toward was making life generally miserable for their bosses by fouling up the reporting. Herb recommended the substitution of a more desirable and constructive reward for accurate, on-time reporting. Herb also suggested steps management could take to improve relationships with the supervisors.

I'd bet that while the supervisors were wreaking vengeance on their bosses, they were getting rewarded with, say, annual merit increases. The annual merit increase is probably management's favorite reward—3 percent, 4 percent, 5 percent, 8 percent, or even more each year—usually at the time of the new budget. But despite management's wishes, the annual merit increases are probably seen by recipients as their rewards for being on the payroll. Since, in most departments, nearly everyone gets something, employees don't see the added money as a recognition of good service—unless of course there is a marked differential. That is, it is well known throughout the department that high performers get 10 percent and that lesser producers get 4 or 5 percent. But when, as is often the case, everyone gets pretty much the same thing, or within the same range, it isn't seen as a reward for much of anything. In one company, employees received a bonus in December. No one was quite sure what the bonus was for since everyone got it. Merit increases followed in January, so it was a glorious time for all. And an expensive time for the company. The act was generous but ineffective in encouraging anything but good feelings. People said, "This is a good place to be." They did not, however, say anything about its being a good place to work, because they saw no connection.

There's another reason why the annual merit increase or a generalized bonus is a poor incentive for working harder and better: the fact that it is annual. People work all year. They get thanked every twelve months. This is literally true in many places. There are no thank yous for the rest of the time. So the annual merit increase is usually too little and too late to affect performance or to be much of a motivator. Herzberg says it is not a motivator at all. Well, I would suggest that if I were performing well, and if my boss were to say to me in October, "Keep up this level of excellence and I'll see that you get a special increase in January," I would probably be motivated to continue to pour it on. Maybe I'd even put more effort into my work. But in January, once I had the raise, it would no longer be a motivator for me. As Herzberg insists, its motivational value would drop to zero. It would become a maintenance factor.

Because the usual wage and salary policies in most organizations militate against money being a potent motivator, I don't talk or write much about it as a reward. For my book *The Manager's Motivation Desk Book,* I developed a list of thirty-seven ways a manager can reward an employee for good performance. Making an employee feel special through belonging to an elite is probably a thirty-eighth.

I firmly believe that managers should create an elite in their departments—an elite of employees who are rewarded for working up to the manager's standards. At this point, managers often express a primal fear: What do I do about the people who don't work up to my standards? This fear, incidentally, is probably one of the common reasons why we continue to encourage mediocre or poor performance. If we as managers insisted on good performance from everyone, we'd have to deal with those who are below the line.

My answer to the fear is to do everything reasonable to help the people who are below the minimally acceptable standard to improve sufficiently, and if that doesn't work, get rid of them. That's painful. Managers for the most part would like to avoid pain. They don't want to hurt people. They want to be seen as nice—a desire that dominates too many managerial behaviors. Of course, these days, there is the threat of a suit for wrongful discharge. If a manager sets clear standards, works with a failing employee, gives feedback, and keeps documentation of his or her efforts, the manager reduces the risk of a successful legal action.

Sometimes I hear in managers' voices a tone of resignation: There will always be, they say, some people at the bottom. That's true, if you grade on the curve. You can indeed create an elite, but you will always have the poor—or so the thinking goes. But why should you?

The truth is this, I've become convinced: Many managers do not really believe they have the right to set reasonable standards of performance and to expect employees to try to work according to them. I do not know why this is true, but I can say the revelation that they have such a right often seems to come as a surprise to them.

Let me be as emphatic as I can: Every manager has the right to expect employees to abide by his or her standards. The standards have to be reasonable, of course. Work that requires an immoderate expenditure of effort and undue risk of failure will discourage employees. But if the manager is convinced that subordinates can, with reasonable effort, meet the standards, the manager is obliged to do two things: Reward the successful efforts by employees and terminate, demote, or transfer the failures.

One note of caution: Once you insist that subordinates do

what you expect (and you must be sure that they know what you expect), and once you determine that you will reward only for performance that is acceptable, you must be consistent, and you must continue to be so. Otherwise you will lose credibility and control. Further, you will find that the new elite you are creating will lose tolerance for your keeping people who will not abide by your standards. Gradually you will indeed create an aristocracy of people who work well and who feel good about what they do. Your department will probably earn the envy of other managers, and no doubt many of their employees will want to work for you.

At that point, giving medals to everyone who performs well makes sense. There will be no debasement of the coin of the realm. We've all been taught that managers shouldn't play favorites. But when it comes to people who perform for you, they deserve every reward you can justify. And people who don't perform should get short shrift.

Chapter 10

SOBs Can Make
Good Bosses, Too

I realize that the trend in management these days is toward participation and workplace democracy, but let's not forget that the great social psychologist Kurt Lewin defined three styles of leadership: authoritarian, democratic, and laissez-faire. All three are legitimate, but we Americans get swept up in currents; the autocrat is out of style.

When I am tempted to believe that being an autocrat is out, I remind myself of the late George Szell, who, at his death, was musical director of the Cleveland Orchestra, generally considered to be one of the top five U.S. symphony orchestras. Szell was not only an autocrat, he was not very likable. Sir Rudolf Bing, director of the Metropolitan Opera in the 1950s and 1960s, wrote that Szell was "a nasty man." On one of his birthdays, the members of the orchestra decided to play a little joke to recognize the day. When he showed for rehearsal, down went the baton, and instead of Beethoven, the strains were those of "Happy Birthday." Szell is said to have scowled throughout the performance, then to have muttered, "Very funny. Now let's work." That was the end of that.

But what George Szell did with the Cleveland Orchestra was to be an effective boss. If you're one of the big five, you're one of the world's best. Every man and woman in that orchestra can play with extra pride, knowing that they are an elite. Szell's superior musicianship and his insistence on the highest standards made it possible for all of the musicians to aim high, to achieve excellence. They are the best, or so close to it that it doesn't matter. You can understand why they felt such loyalty to a man they probably didn't have great affection for. One guest conductor later said that when he stepped onto the podium, he felt as if he were facing "100 little Szells."

Perhaps they didn't all love Szell, but they probably would have followed him anywhere.

Other demanding autocrats come to mind. Also in the musical world was Toscanini, well known for his exacting standards and the displays of temper when they weren't met. George S. Patton, Jr. has become almost a legend of an autocrat, but many of his troops in World War II virtually worshipped him—and did follow him anywhere. Harold Geneen of ITT was very demanding. The joke about his monthly meeting with his executives was his greeting: "Good morning, gentlemen. We'll break for lunch at midnight." Yet, his executive corps was the breeding ground for CEOs for corporations all over the United States.

Most of us in managing like to be admired and respected, and although we don't admit it, we probably want to be loved as well. Our need for affection often gets in the way of doing things we must do to be effective managers—things such as setting high standards and insisting on their being met. When they aren't, we must be prompt and tough in letting employees know they have to shape up or else. And when they don't, we must take the ultimate step and fire. But all of those actions involve pain for both the employees and for the managers. People who inflict pain may not be liked, so we hesitate to do so. But when we don't do our job, ironically, we may wind up not being liked *or* respected.

Probably the most personal sentiment most autocrats crave is loyalty, not affection. They understand the importance of the quid pro quo, however. In fact, the relationship between an SOB and employees works best in situations such as the following.

Emergencies. The company is in trouble and needs a fast turn-around. People feel they need a leader who can see his or her way out of the mess. Employees are very likely to acquiesce to a person who seems to fit that description.

Confusion. The company has sustained weak or uncertain leadership for some time. Employees are fed up with management's indecisiveness. Along comes a rescuer who provides confidence and certainty, the latter being in very short supply. People will invest their trust in such a person.

Lack of Vision. Employees believe they have been working for indifferent or mediocre management. Their pride has no place to go. They know they are capable of achieving more for the company, but management has held them back through misplaced emphases and wrong priorities. A new boss promises excitement through his or her vision and the opportunity for job satisfaction. People are inclined to follow such a visionary.

Exceptional Opportunity. An executive announces to the troops that, because of their new product or service or concept, they all have a chance to be owners and to get rich. Something akin to that happened at People Express, the airline, although the trust placed in top management may not have been warranted—employees didn't get rich, for the most part. But for a while there was a lot of hard work.

There are other reasons—perhaps as many as there are people who are willing to work for an autocrat, who, while unpleasant, offers other rewards. The individual might be personally compelling—charismatic, to use another term. It's exciting to work for him or her. Charismatic individuals sometimes offer causes in which people can involve themselves. Or perhaps the boss is a very attractive public figure. You can gain prestige just by being associated with the celebrity. Or the boss is a genius. There is much of value that employees can learn reporting to him or her.

But there can be a downside to working for the strict, demanding, even obnoxious autocrat. The following are examples.

Limited Growth and Opportunity. Autocrats are often quite turf-minded; they may not take kindly to threats and competition. The most virulent response to an external threat may occur in the form of an ambitious or talented subordinate, and it often comes later in life when it would seem that the autocrat should have become comfortable and confident. Someone makes an attempt to take more authority or responsibility, and the autocrat's wrath is fearsome. I would find it depressing to keep bumping up against someone's fear or pride.

The Assumption of All Wisdom. One of the joys of working in a democratic or participative environment is the recognition that resources exist throughout the organization and that they are utilized frequently. People join together in making decisions that affect themselves and the well-being of the company. There are sensors throughout the company that react to changes from within and from without. There are many perspectives on where the company is and where it might go.

It's difficult for me to believe that, no matter how brilliant and talented, one person could even begin to substitute for the collective wisdom of the entire organization. Yet, the autocrat often demands that the major decisions are reserved for that eminent personage. As a result, his or her successors are usually not experienced or independent enough to take over. Look at the convulsions of the airline industry when some of the founding fathers finally stepped aside. It's possible that Pan Am and Eastern never have recovered from the trauma.

Devaluation of People. Recently I watched a television interview with an executive who stoutly declared, "I'm tough, but I'm fair." The camera followed her around during her business day and confirmed what she said: She was indeed tough and fair; in her world, fairness meant equality. Everyone got the same humiliating treatment. I feel that my dignity is at stake when another person believes that he or she has the right to dictate to me, to embarrass me, or to talk down to me. I have a strong objection to being treated like chattel.

Many autocrats, I suspect, operate on Theory X assumptions about their employees—that they would really prefer not to work and that they must be coerced, threatened with punishment, controlled, and followed about in order to get work out of them. Such bosses are often paternalistic, seeing their employees as children. Paternalism characterized many corporations until recent years. Give me loyalty and obedience, and I will take care of you, the father says. But with grown people, paternalism is a devaluation of their dignity.

The above are some of the pros and cons of working for an autocrat, who may even be an SOB and still practice effective management. That is, he or she gets the desired results from people. They can be good bosses—for some. They can satisfy the needs—of some. But, I'd wager, most people would find autocratic bosses to wear thin over time, to be constrictive, and to be too possessive.

But in partial rebuttal, I must say that every manager should be prepared to play the role of an autocrat when it is appropriate. It may not be popular, but it is realistic. There will be people who justify Theory X assumptions. There will be emergencies and earthshaking changes. There will be opportunities to be seized. And there will always be a need for vision. In short, there will always be appropriate moments for a strong leader. Even an SOB.

Chapter 11

Most People Don't Resist Change, But Victims Do

A persistent, self-serving belief held by many managements is that people resist change. It's convenient for management to believe that. The belief justifies manipulation and propaganda designed to convince employees that change will actually benefit them in the long run—contrary to evidence that the change will hurt them. When change has been introduced and people discover that the change has not been in their best interest and when they discover that, in all likelihood, management has lied, the victims most likely will not again believe management when they say, "This won't hurt a bit." And the next time, they'll resist the change—as management predicted they would.

In short, people don't resist change. They resist what they fear is being done to them. And they're usually right.

People's paranoia is pervasive. A few years ago, commuters who rode the Long Island Railroad showed up at the Manhattan terminal to find that train employees had walked out that afternoon. No one could get information about anything. One woman tried to call her family, but the pay phone took her money, wouldn't complete the call, and wouldn't return her money. "You see," she sighed to a newspaper reporter who was standing nearby, "if they don't get you one way, they get you another." Of course, while her paranoia is almost funny, it's helpful to remember the old caution: Just because you're paranoid doesn't mean the bastards *aren't* out to get you.

For most people, the culprits are management. One wishes management, in their announcements of change, would be only mildly dishonest, such as many doctors are. When a doctor assures you that "this will cause you some discomfort," you can bet that it's going to hurt like hell. So when the doctor says, "I'm afraid this is going to hurt," you know you're in deep trouble.

But management insists that this is not going to hurt. Well, it may look as if it will, but, trust us, it's only a cosmetic or superficial thing. A number of years ago, a company announced that, instead of paying its employees every two weeks, it would start paying them weekly. In order for the system to be changed to the new schedule, no one would receive a salary for the week after Christmas. It would be made up at the end of the next year. Soon there were clusters of agitated employees commiserating with one another about not getting any money during what is perhaps the most costly time of the year for most people.

A delegation went to top management and pointed out the severe inconvenience. Management's representative shrugged his shoulders and said, "I don't know what the fuss is all about. No one is going to lose any money. There will be fifty-two pay periods in the new year." The delegation agreed, but stubbornly pointed out that people would have expenses to pay during the holiday period and that it was not the best time of the year to ask for sacrifices. Finally, management grudgingly made an accommodation, but it doesn't take much imagination to anticipate the employees' reactions to the next memo saying that there would be a small change in the system that no one needs to worry about.

Ironically, the change to weekly payment proved to be one of the most popular policies ever instituted. But management had taken a lot of pleasure out of it.

Another game that management likes to play in announcing change is to rationalize the reason for it, even though the reason publicized probably has nothing to do with anything. When I was a young salesman in charge of the New Jersey group insurance office for a large insurance company, I suffered from a severe personality conflict with the company's general agent. Unknown to me, the general agent was feeding the home office with all sorts of complaints about how I did this or didn't do that. Management had just about decided that I would have to be let go when it occurred to them to ask me whether I had any last words before the blindfolding. I told them that I had known nothing about the backstairs gossiping. At that point they admitted some culpability in taking someone else's word exclusively, and they suggested that perhaps, since the conflict looked unsolvable, I might wish to transfer to the newly opened New York office. Shortly after I'd gotten settled across the river, I received a letter from my ultimate boss, a vice president, telling me that they had decided to offer me the new post to provide me with growth opportunities. To put it mildly, the letter did not increase management's credibility. They had goofed and they found a smooth way out of a rough problem. But none of that apparently had anything to do with the transfer.

A move out of desperation, as in my case, is often announced as an exciting innovation. For a number of years, I followed the history of another company's sales force, fascinated that every three or four years salespeople had to endure systemic convulsions. When this first came to my attention, the company had two separate field forces, each selling its own product line. But the results hadn't been profitable. So, under pressure from top management, the sales manager announced an exciting, promising new plan. They would combine the sales forces and the product lines, and every field person would make a ton of money. Three years later, again as a result of prodding, the sales manager waxed enthusiastic about a great new innovation: They were going to break up the sales force to create two groups of specialists, each with its own product lines.

You might wonder how they got away with their cycles. One thing that saved the sales manager was that top management was incompetent. They didn't know anything about selling, so they relied on the sales manager—even though, to borrow from the French, he was the devil they knew. Another reason their merry-go-round escaped detection was the 100 percent turnover of salespeople in each three-year period. Between the incompetence of the field leadership and the lack of opportunity to make money, there was little incentive to hang around. But you can bet that the inside employees, who did hang around, gave little credence to the memos issuing from the field sales department.

But, remembering the woman caught in the rail strike, the lack of trust, even paranoia, is widely justified in our society. It isn't just a matter of management's conning its employees. Seemingly, everyone does it to everyone else. To illustrate, I recently received a letter from the publisher of a specialized magazine I subscribe to. I found the magazine very helpful in some professional work I was doing. Here is part of the letter:

> Your professional success is the rationale behind every issue of _____ that we prepare. That's why we take your suggestions for future articles very seriously. Fortunately, or unfortunately, the response from you as to research projects you'd like us to report on has been heavier than anticipated, which is gratifying. However, to provide you with the very best written, comprehensive articles we can, we're going to take more time to do the job even better. And we're going to give you even more time to take advantage of the articles you've requested from us. You'll have more time to assess your needs, and we'll have more time to fashion our magazine to those needs.
>
> That's why we're changing _____ from a monthly to a bimonthly. With this change, you'll have everything to gain and nothing to lose.

Sure. When I read the above, I thought about the time my five-year-old son was persuaded to have his tonsils out for health reasons. When he came to, he wailed, "I want my tonsils back." I'm sympathetic. The publisher mentioned nothing about my continuing to pay the twelve-issue rate even though I'll get only six.

Is it any wonder people resist change when the change agents sound like pitchmen: "Tell ya what I'm gonna do." Even if managements have short memories, their employees don't. Remember Santayana: Those who cannot remember the past are condemned to fulfill it.

Let's examine the myth that people resist change. Obviously, according to this belief, most people would be very happy if nothing new happened to shake up their lives. A few years ago, a sales manager asked me what he should do about a former high producer who had plateaued. Nothing would move him to do more than he had to in order to keep his job. I asked the sales manager, "How long has this man been doing essentially what he is doing now?" The answer: "Fifteen years." So I put the questions, "Would you like to do essentially the same thing for fifteen years? I doubt it. Why then do you think he would be content?" The sales manager had an unmotivated salesman and didn't recognize it.

Frederick Herzberg established almost thirty years ago that certain kinds of changes motivate people: advancement, possibility for growth, new tasks, new assignments, and new responsibilities. Not only do employees have a tolerance for such changes, according to Herzberg's research (which is now pretty well accepted without challenge), they get turned on by them. How great an intellectual leap would it be to suggest that they will not automatically resist change if they find certain changes in their work and life to be attractive? And this means any change, as long as they can see a rationale for it and even though they might suffer from the consequences. For example, in a number of industries and companies, we've recently seen employees consent to a reduction in their pay and other benefits to keep their plants open or to avoid substantial cutbacks in people.

Maybe those employees who accepted less money didn't like it, but they nonetheless accepted it. And the resentment was often less when they were brought into the decision-making process; the change was not simply imposed on them. More than thirty years ago, Rensis Likert researched participative styles of management, and claimed that people work better and more productively if they are brought into the decision making that will affect them. Likert's System 4 represented, he argued, the kind of organization that people he surveyed said would be the most desirable in which to work and the most effective in getting results. Here's my description of System 4: Management trusts employees, regards them as working willingly toward the achievement of organizational objectives. People are motivated by rewards. At all levels they are involved in discussing and deciding those issues that are important to them. Communication is quite accurate and goes up, down, and across. Goals are not ordered from on high but are set with the participation of the people who will have to work to achieve them.

Informal organizations are benign—they support the formal organization.

Is this a profile of your organization? If it is, you exist among a happy minority of employees. The most advanced organization that I have ever had contact with is what Likert describes as System 3—consultative. Management keeps control but sometimes consults with employees. Management still makes the decisions, but communication is cautious, and unpleasant or unfavorable information is not freely offered by anyone.

You'd think that in the 1980s we would have come further since Douglas McGregor enunciated his Theory X and Theory Y thirty years ago (wonder why so much wonderful stuff emerged three decades ago?). Back then, as I recall, no one wanted to be a so-called Theory X manager. It was terribly unfashionable. But there's not much doubt that Theory X assumptions about people still abound; they are alive and well and living in top management. Just to refresh your mind, here's the way McGregor describes the traditional way of looking at employees: (1) The average human being has an inherent dislike of work and will avoid it if he can. (2) Because of this characteristic dislike of work, most people must be coerced, controlled, directed, threatened with punishment to get them to put forth adequate effort toward the achievement of organizational objectives. (3) The average human being prefers to be directed, wishes to avoid responsibility, has relatively little ambition, wants security above all.

It's easy, rereading McGregor's profile, to understand how a management that accepts this profile would believe that if people didn't like the work as it is, they probably won't like work the way it's going to become after a few changes. So, the reasoning goes, let's make it as easy for everyone as we can. Let's not demoralize our folks any further. Besides, they really don't deserve to be considered an essential part of this organization, as we managers are.

Management doesn't trust employees. And employees don't trust management. And when the lady doesn't get her money back from the telephone, she feels as if *they* got her, one way or the other.

Once in a while, though, you hear a nice little story about a manager who, facing a big problem or even a potential catastrophe, says to employees, "It's about to hit the fan. Here's what is happening, and here is what might. Let's not spend a lot of time trying to pin the blame. That won't help now. But what will help is your sitting down with me and figuring out how we can save ourselves." They do both because, you see, they probably know the operation a lot better than people upstairs or in the front office. And in the process, the employees become *they*. There is no longer any reason for anyone to distrust anyone again.

Maybe they didn't live happily ever after, but one hopes they lived truthfully ever after. The truth shall make you free, the adage goes. I just wish that many managements accepted that as true. Then the rest of us could get on with the business of coping with change, which goes on all the time, regardless.

Part Three

RELATING TO OTHERS
AS EQUALS

*T*here's a widespread implication in management that as you grow older or acquire more knowledge and experience, you become more confident in your abilities to evaluate and to decide. Your judgment becomes tempered and firmer. In reality, as you grow older and presumably gain in wisdom, you become aware that your perceptions and judgments on their own may be quite suspect. Younger managers and professionals often find it threatening to seek the perceptions and opinions of others, or even to accept that those who differ from them have a right to hold those differences. Wiser people say, "This is what I believe to be true, but maybe I'd better check reality by finding out how others see and feel." In short, you are an expert in your perceptions and feelings, and that's all. You have to ask and to involve others to find out whether they agree with you.

Customer service, about which I write in this section, is a good example. We've all heard the old adage "The customer is always right." Well, I doubt that most of us really believe that. In fact, the customer is often wrong. But the customer doesn't believe he or she is wrong, which is what the adage is telling us. We don't have to agree with the customer, but we do have to accept the customer's perceptions of the situation. Traditionally, in management development, the difference between acceptance and agreement, so vital to good communications, has not been emphasized.

And as any good salesperson knows, you can't hope to persuade anyone to accept what you have to offer without your understanding the other person's needs and wants and how what you have can meet those needs. In short, this section is largely about your getting outside yourself to check reality, to relate better with others, and to open up your boundaries.

As I suggested in the previous section, we need our partnerships with others. And those partnerships don't work without equality of the partners.

Chapter 12

Using Your Fallibility
to Build Your Credibility

I once knew an executive who was never wrong. To be more precise, he thought he was never wrong. And when people who worked with him suggested that something he did or said seemed at variance with a previous decision or action, he always provided an explanation, sometimes tortured, to show that the disparity existed only in their minds. He valued his credibility—and every person should—but he believed that one built credibility by not making mistakes, or, at least, by not admitting mistakes.

Life's joke, of course, was on him, because no one with whom he dealt expected him to be infallible. In fact, no one believed he could be. So he failed to gain the very credibility he strove for and sometimes twisted himself like a pretzel for.

However, the pressure to be infallible sometimes comes from without. Others may have a need for us to be perfectly consistent with everything we previously have done or have said. The well-know psychologist George Kelly once conducted a brief seminar for graduate students at a southern university. I have been told that after giving a lengthy answer to a student's question, Kelly was confronted by another student who said, "You've just contradicted yourself. On page such-and-such of your book"—he held it up—"you wrote . . . " And the student read from the paragraph. There was a long silence. Many of the other students were embarrassed by the aggressive tone of the critic. Finally, Kelly answered, quietly, "I feel insulted that you think I cannot learn anything new."

The logical projection from that anecdote is not the more learning that takes place, the less consistent a person is. I once had a colleague who was much given to uttering periodic profoundities that often veered sharply away from those she had spoken previously. I called them "the eternal verity for the week." But I suspect the truth is that a person who is almost totally consistent hasn't learned much of anything. That person is in a deep rut. When I was a young man growing up in a small midwestern town, I remember hearing people say that they voted Democratic or Republican— more likely the latter—because "my father voted that way." That's the kind of consistency that, fortunately, has pretty much disappeared.

Where does one draw the line on this issue? How much fallibility can people take before one's credibility suffers? I doubt very much that it's a question of how often you make a mistake. Rather, it's a matter of how you present yourself when you make a statement or a decision. The greater the certitude you display as to the consequences—as to how right you are—the greater the risk your credibility will suffer should you be wrong.

As a trainer and consultant, my credibility has to be one of my important assets. At the same time, there is no need for me to present myself as promulgating laws or as dictating the one way to do things right. In fact, I'd soon lose my credibility if that were my behavior. In managing, there are no laws, and there is no one way to do things right. So I present my views as what they are: This is the way I would do it. Thus, I don't put my credibility on the line, and I don't lose it by a bad throw of the dice.

Sometimes admitting a mistake can later serve to increase your credibility. A remarkable example of this truth is in the letter that President Lincoln wrote to General Grant after the latter took Vicksburg in July 1863. Lincoln used his fallibility with no fear that he himself would be reduced in stature but with the probable hope that Grant's stature would be increased.

> My dear general: I do not remember that you and I ever met personally. I write this now as a grateful acknowledgment for the almost inestimable service you have done the country. I wish to say a word further. When you first reached the vicinity of Vicksburg, I thought you should do what you finally did— march the troops across the neck, run the batteries with the transports, and thus go below; and I never had any faith, except a general hope that you knew better than I, that the

Yazoo Pass expedition and the like could succeed. When you got below and took Port Gibson, Grang Gulf and vicinity, I thought you should go down the river and join General Banks, and when you turned northward, east of the Big Black, I feared it was a mistake. I now wish to make the personal acknowledgment that you were right and I was wrong.

The letter was an extraordinary way to express gratitude for some superb soldiering. Grant, by taking Vicksburg, had gained a strategic victory for the Union by cutting the Confederacy in two and making the Mississippi fully navigable for northern river trade. Subsequent relations between Lincoln and Grant demonstrate without question that Lincoln's credibility with Grant never suffered. Interestingly, more than a year later, Grant suffered a tragic setback at Petersburg when the Union troops mined the Confederate lines and created a trap for themselves. Grant assumed the responsibility and, so far as we know, lost none of the credence Lincoln gave him.

At the same time that Vicksburg fell, Robert E. Lee was defeated at Gettysburg. Lee was driven to fight in the small Pennsylvania town by desperation: he needed a victory that would have diplomatic and psychological consequences for the South. If he won, he sensed that some European nations were ready to extend diplomatic recognition to the Confederacy and that the Union might be ready to sue for peace. But desperation often produces miserable decisions. On the third day, Lee sent Pickett's troops across the fields to attack the well-entrenched Union troops on Cemetery Hill, losing thousands of good men. Lee accepted the blame for the bad judgment that led to the slaughter. Although Pickett never forgave the old man, all the evidence shows that his troops continued to love Lee fervently.

Assuming responsibility for a misjudgment is simply good damage control. If too much certitude before a mistake can be a blunder, so is stubbornness afterward. Several years ago, a famous manufacturer of consumer products highly touted their significant breakthrough in producing a battery-powered lawn mower. I bought one, relying on the name and reputation of the company, but it was a lemon. When I took it into the factory-authorized service shop, the representative said, "Get your money back." "You can't fix it? It's only a couple of months old." "Get your money back," he repeated. I concluded from the way he talked that I wasn't the only man who'd bought a lemon.

I wrote a nice letter of complaint to the company to ask for a refund. And somewhere in it I commiserated with them for having produced such a disappointing mower. It had, after all, been a terrific idea. The answer, from a vice president, turned aside my commiseration. Yes, it had been and continued to be a terrific idea. He was sorry that I'd had a bad experience with it, but all across the country people were simply delighted with their new mowers. Nonetheless he would be happy to refund the entire amount.

It was a silly exercise. His letter was entirely incredible. Apparently his public relations people had convinced him that he must stonewall it. And, as a public relations gesture, it failed. It put me off that company for years. I didn't like being told that I was wrong about the whole thing. The mistake was theirs, not mine. (It *was* a mistake: the product was withdrawn.) Something like the following would have impressed me favorably: "We're sorry that you've had problems with our new model. It's important to us that you believe we stand behind our fine products; we want you to continue to think well of us. Here is the purchase price in full. Thank you for letting us know so that we can serve you better."

"Never explain, never complain," goes the saying. There is no defensive explanation in the above text, and there isn't a hint of petulance. What I received instead was the usual kind of customer service that offends and erodes my trust. The psychological advantage to saying those magic three words, "We are sorry," is that people are disarmed. They expect the person who may have made the mistake to be defensive, to sputter, to rationalize, to justify. But no, he or she simply says, "I'm sorry." Even better, "What can I do to rectify things?"

The classic case that should occupy a leading chapter in every text on customer service and marketing is the Tylenol poisoning situation. The company was not at fault, but they did not try to soften things by explanations and assurances. They simply ordered all boxes of the product off the shelf. The message that the consumer received was, "We value you so much that we will take a loss of hundreds of millions of dollars to prevent anyone else from being hurt."

"We are sorry." Most customer service complaints could be laid to rest if those three words became part of the vocabulary in business. And the same results are available to a manager who has made a poor decision in good faith. "I am sorry. I have goofed."

Well, all that's good for helping to clean up the mess, the reader says. But what I really need is to be able to cut down on the incidence of mistakes and failure so that I don't have to apologize. I want to increase my credibility, the manager says, by cutting down on my fallibility. Here are some suggestions.

Take Time. As I've written elsewhere, decisiveness is not necessarily good decision making. There is the usual pressure to resolve an ambiguity. Go one way or the other. But the truth is that many decisions don't have to be made as quickly as they are; it is not so much the demands of the situation as it is the pressure on the decider.

Fast decisions may be rational, but slower decisions are nonrational (not irrational) as well as rational. Intuition and emotions come into play, and they provide the wisdom that logic alone may lack. Consider how often you've made up your mind at ten o'clock at night only to awaken at six in the morning realizing that you must go the opposite way. That's because your nonrational faculties have been working for you. As I'm fond of saying, let your gut do the deciding. It's much more reliable than your analytical brain. The analytical brain is often dominated by shoulds, whereas your intuition is guided by wants and needs.

Involve Others. One person's perspective can be narrowly focused; it's either this or that. But decisions seldom involve only two options. Other people bring other perspectives, other options. Managers often cut others out because they don't want to hear additional options. But the soundest and most lasting decisions are those in which the greatest number of choices have been generated and evaluated. Besides, if the decision involves the department, chances are that others know certain aspects of the operation much better than the manager. The more people involved, the greater the chance that the manager will hear a possibility he or she hadn't considered.

Monitor Indicators. What will tell you when you have made a good decision? What will be the red or yellow flags? Too many people make decisions and feel locked in by them: "We must see this through." But it was Peter Drucker, I think, who said that the only good decision is one that can be reversed. If you feel you are on an unchangeable course, you have something to worry about even if the indicators are good.

And what if the indicators are not good? Well, don't be the poker player who says, "If I hang on for another round, maybe my luck will change." Step in. Take control. Announce, "This is not working," or, "I'm sorry, I've made a mistake. I need help to correct it." And in most cases people will help. They hadn't expected you to be infallible to begin with.

A child will deny a mistake because the child thinks only of an immediate sanction, such as a scolding. One of my fondest memories is the little boy in my house who soiled his pants, and, when confronted with the evidence, said stoutly, although tearfully, "I didn't do it."

As adults, we are in this thing—whatever it may be—for the long run. The immediate pain or embarrassment is not what guides us. It's how people will see us, not only now but in the future. They don't see us as infallible. They see us as responsible—able to admit our mistakes. These days the management textbooks sometimes forget the wisdom of General Motors' Sloan: A manager who is right half the time is doing well indeed.

Chapter 13

Outvoting the
Lone Dissenter
May Be Dangerous

*I*n American folklore, the lone figure standing up against the many has assumed mythic proportions—the dissenting hero, championing an unpopular cause or not backing away from responsibility. One can't help thinking of Gary Cooper in *High Noon* as his townspeople distanced themselves from him when he tried to enlist their help to defend the town against the gunslingers who were about to invade it.

The harsh truth is that the Gary Coopers may loom tall on the screen, but they really aren't welcome in the corporate conference room. Americans say they like the maverick and appreciate the dissenter. But when a decision is about to be made, the fellow who says, "I'm not convinced that we should do this," "I'm not sure I understand what we're doing," or "I have a problem with what is going on," is seldom a hero. Others around the table may look at him as a troublemaker, just as the sheriff's townspeople did.

A young manager was telling me the other day about his experience in just such a group. His boss was away, and he was expected to sit in for her in any meetings she would normally attend. In one such meeting, the field marketing department had a proposal they wanted to present to some of the department managers. The man representing his boss listened carefully and found a number of projected steps in the proposal that he disagreed with, based on his earlier years as a salesman. He voiced his objections. There was a moment of silence, and then the marketing director said, "This is not up for a decision. We've already made up our minds that we're going to do this." A few days later, another meeting was called to explain more details about the plan. The dissenter was told that he need not attend. The project ran into many of the problems he anticipated.

Isolating the dissenter, as was done in the case of the young manager, is one way decision makers can deal with someone who disagrees with a proposed action. Probably a more common method of quashing dissent is to explain carefully to the holdout the rationale for the decision. Most likely, the rationale was quite clear before, but it is repeated, as if the dissenter were a dummy, incapable of understanding what everyone else presumably grasped easily. And there may even be a conscious effort to make the objector feel stupid; it can be an effective disarming tactic. Then someone will call for a vote, the dissenter will be handily outvoted, and people will file out of the room without looking at him. They are embarrassed for him, but they should be embarrassed because of him; he may be telling them something they should know.

When I was a young group insurance salesman, the industry introduced what is now known as catastrophic or major medical coverage. Since it was an innovation, no one really knew what form it should take or how much it should cost. Each time one of our competitors came up with a slightly different design for the coverage, we field people clamored to be able to sell something just like it, for competitive reasons. It was a time of craziness for a normally sedate industry.

My company's plans and premiums were quite reasonable, and I saw a terrific opportunity to get a lot of business. One plan I especially liked was a simple but comprehensive approach: The insured paid the first $25 of expenses due to an illness or accident, then the insurance company paid the next $500 in full for hospital, surgery, doctors' calls, prescriptions, and so forth, after which the coverage was 80 percent of covered expenses to a maximum of $5,000 or $10,000. These days that protection doesn't seem so extravagant. But in the 1950s, a hospital stay with surgery might add up to less than $1,000.

For a time, I took advantage of the new plans, selling them quite merrily without any sense of danger. One day, however, I received a proposal for the major medical coverage I described above for a small company that had very basic hospital and surgical protection: $8 per day for room and board for thirty-five days (adequate insurance for those days), with a surgical schedule that had a maximum of $200. The monthly major medical family premium was one cent higher than the plan the company already had. The bell went off. It didn't seem to me that it was prudent to offer many times the insurance protection for the same money. So I wrote to the group actuary, suggesting that our major medical premiums might be a bit low. I supported my premise with two or three other examples. Back came a letter advising me that the actuarial department had done much research and had considered carefully before devising the rates. They believed that their work was sound.

In short, get off our turf. Mind your own business. Well, of course, I had the naive notion that my business was theirs and vice versa. I shrugged and sold a lot more of that bargain. Within a year, about the time of the first renewals, many premiums jumped 100 percent because of heavy claims, and the more liberal plans were discontinued. We would eventually lose millions.

I must say that the group actuary, in a subsequent meeting, was gracious in telling everyone that I had warned them. But in defending their turf, they had failed to consider the possibility that we might wind up losing a great deal of money.

The above are examples of three familiar techniques for silencing a dissenter: Isolate the person, outvote him or her, or suggest that the person is out-of-bounds, which translates into "You can't know what you're talking about." We may respect the role that Gary Cooper played. We just don't want his kind working for us.

Yet, he may not stand alone. He may in fact have a constituency—an important consideration if your action or decision affects others. In our weekly editorial meetings at the Research Institute of America, all the copy for all our newsletters underwent examination by all of the staff. If someone said about a piece of copy, "I don't understand this point," or "I'm not sure I agree with this point," the flag raiser was listened to carefully. It was considered bad form for any other staff member, especially the writer of the piece, to respond, "I have no problem understanding it," or "It works for me." We recognized that if one editor had reservations about the copy, some of our subscribers would as well. The rule was, therefore, satisfy the questioner, and you'll avoid problems with your readers. That principle holds true when you make decisions affecting not only your customers but also your employees. If someone suggests that a new policy might create resistance from subordinates, listen. You may be able to head off a lot of bad feelings later. Consider yourself lucky that you had advance notice.

But a dissenter may have a constituency in the room as well. Some decisions are made but don't stay made. When someone in the meeting has a reservation about the decision, don't automatically jump to its defense and try to talk him or her out of the objection. The fact is that there are often others in the group who share the questioner's concern but don't speak up. The harder you argue against the dissenter, the more intimidated these people might become. Instead, you need to encourage these others to talk as well and to help them realize that they don't stand alone. Otherwise, you may have to convene another session later to undo the decision and make another one.

Cognitive dissonance may also force you to hold a follow-up meeting. People may develop some questions after they leave the conference room; it is quite normal to wonder whether you have, in fact, made the right decision. Watch people study the interest ads after they've committed their money to a CD. They want to be assured that they put the money with the right institution. The process they're going through is called *harmonization*. If they succeed in convincing themselves that they made the right choice, everything is fine. But if they don't, they're unhappy. When people walk out of your meeting, they may experience dissonance, and, if they do, they will seek harmony. The dissenter in the meeting, whom you may have dismissed as a loner, now has a constituency.

The occasional dissenter should not be regarded as being in the same class as, in my terms, the professional devil's advocate. There are people who seem to derive their power by nay saying. Indeed, there is a lot of power in the word *no* in many meetings. People are uncertain about what to do, or they are uncomfortable discussing the issue (which probably means that it desperately needs to be worked through). Into the midst of the uncertainty and anxiety steps the person who always sees issues from the negative side. "I don't think this will work," "We tried this before without success," or "I really don't believe that management will go for it." It might be a mild demurral, such as, "Why don't we table this and talk about it next spring?" Everyone breathes a sigh of relief and agrees. Being negative is the way some people achieve visibility. At one academic meeting I attended, a professor frequently started his speeches by saying, "I am troubled by . . ." After about four such openings, I entertained myself by imagining all the ways I thought the group could add to his troubles.

Yes, you must consider the source. At the same time, the chronic nay sayer may, for the first time, have a solid point. In all cases of dissent, therefore, the wise meeting chair will insist on a full discussion of the reservation. The final group action will probably be better for having aired any potential problems inherent in the action.

Of course, a lot of postdecision problems can be avoided by abandoning the cherished majority rule and converting to consensus decisions. Consensus decisions take longer, but they usually generate more options and they certainly result in a higher level of ownership. No one leaves the room until he or she is committed to the decision. It saves a lot of time later.

We pride ourselves on being a society with free speech, but in reality, we don't much care for speech that is too free—speech that disagrees. So, Gary, when you strap on your gun, perhaps we should *all* strap on our guns.

Chapter 14

Advancing a
Revolutionary Idea:
Courtesy to Customers

*T*here's a misanthropic movement afoot to discourage the use of the phrase "Have a nice day." One of my friends, who is vehemently opposed to hearing those words, replies, "Thank you, but I've made other plans." Let me go on record: I like to have someone wish me a nice day; I think it is an oasis of civility in a world that is turning out to be as unfriendly as the Sahara. We call ourselves a service economy, but increasingly, as customers, we may wonder where the service is.

I once saw in a newsclip Tom Peters, the author, consultant, and, when it comes to customer service, evangelist, say to an audience, "I'm not asking you to love your customers; just don't hate them." The starkness of that wisdom makes it unconventional, in my book.

It's not that I often feel hated, but I do sense frequently that I am an intrusion. If it were not for me, the message goes, the people I interrupt would have a much smoother existence. The other day I returned a spoiled chicken to the supermarket where I've been a customer for a dozen years. I approached the manager's desk— actually it's a balcony. I stood there, looking up, hoping to get the assistant's attention. Finally, she glared at me. "Yes?" I thought, if I were manager of this store, I would not want everyone here to know that I sell rotten chickens, so I spoke softly. I held up the bag and said, in a quiet voice, "This chicken is going bad." "What?" she barked. Oh, to hell with it, I thought. "This chicken smells," I answered, in a loud voice. She reached down for it, took the bag, and sniffed it, which I found offensive. My credibility was zero. I got my money back, but, for some reason, I kept smelling that putrid chicken all day—or was it the discourteous service?

The other day I needed a notary public, and I usually can find one at a bank. I went to the service desk of the branch where I've been a customer for many years and asked, "Do you have a notary?" The woman glanced at me for an instant, then looked down, shuffled some papers, and said, "No, we don't." I was struck by the lack of civility in the response. Here I was, a customer, asking for service. It wasn't her fault there is no notary in the branch, but why couldn't she say, "I'm sorry, we don't." She had to tell a customer the bank couldn't provide a service. Shouldn't she regret that?

I called a fish market to order some oysters for my Thanksgiving stuffing. I've never dealt with these folks before. The clerk took my order on the telephone, said brusquely, "You got it," and hung up. No "Thanks for calling."

I realize that some people will read this and say, "Well, what can he expect if he insists on living in New York City? Everyone knows that New Yorkers are cold and rude." That's not true. New Yorkers are some of the warmest people you'd ever want to meet. In fact, I find their warmth to be much more genuine than that of people in other places who may greet me—a perfect stranger—as if we were at a Lions Club lunch.

No, I'm talking about the decline in simple courtesy when dealing with customers. And that decline must be evident outside of New York City; otherwise Tom Peters wouldn't be making so much money crisscrossing the country, selling the idea of being civilized with the people whose money you take.

I have some rather simple solutions to many of our customer service problems. The first is to reward managers for being decent to customers. I'm not sure many companies do that. I agree with Peters: You don't have to have affection for me, but a little respect will do just fine. If you reward managers for being nice, you'll find an amazing truth: Their subordinates also will be more likely to be nice to customers. It starts at the top. I occasionally patronize a rather expensive store despite the surliness of the sales people there, and I know where their attitude came from. If you stop the manager to ask him a question, he looks at you as if you had spoiled his day.

In such an atmosphere, employees know that they'll earn no brownie points by being pleasant to customers.

In contrast, I frequently used to eat lunch at a restaurant across the street from my office. (I like to tell this story to restaurateurs in New York, where the attrition rate of new restaurants is about 50 percent the first year after opening.) The food was good, but I was a customer there because they treated me specially. The owner always greeted me by name, and he looked as though he was happy to see me. His waitresses, most of whom had been there for years (that tells you something) also greeted me by name and often stopped by my table to chat. Not only did Phil seem to like his customers (whether he did or not), he would not have tolerated shoddy service or disrespect on the part of any employee.

Be nice to customers, and they'll be nice to you. Half of midtown Manhattan practically wept when Phil decided he wanted the more leisurely life of a country restaurant.

My second prescription for effective customer service—which means that you deal with customers in such a way that they keep coming back—is that all problems get the initial response of, "We're sorry." I suspect that many businesspeople are reluctant to say these two or three words because they may imply that the company or store or bank is responsible for the problem. But they don't. They show that the businessperson simply accepts that the customer believes he or she has a problem. The words say, in effect, "We're sorry that you feel you have a problem." Acceptance of a person's perception is not the same as agreeing with it. The acceptance extends as far as, "I accept the fact that you feel that way." Acceptance is not a form of surrender or of admitting anything. It is a basic human courtesy: You're a person, and you have certain opinions or beliefs, and I accept that you have the right to have them.

In today's uncivil world, people don't expect that kind of respect, and they are usually disarmed when they get it. That's another reason why "We're sorry" is so effective. It lets the customers know I'm not going to suspect them of trying to take advantage of me (remember the woman who smelled the chicken) and that I don't think they are dunderheads who need to be scolded and put in their places. No, I'm going to treat them like human beings. (Of course, I may be giving them the benefit of the doubt, but . . .)

My third recommendation for improving customer service is that all conversations contain the magic words, "Thank you (for telling, for calling, and so on)." No, I am not going to try to make you feel as if you've just walked into my parlor with cow manure on your boots. Instead, I want you to know that you have done me a big favor by letting me know when you've been unhappy with me. That way I have a chance to make you feel good about doing business with me, after all.

The final recommendation in my customer service program is that managers be rewarded for problems they solve. It's not enough to be nice and congenial. You must also solve customers' problems—the sooner, the better. If managers are rewarded on the basis of service cases closed satisfactorily, then you can be sure they'll keep after the employees handling the problems.

There you have my simple formula for improving your customer service: (1) Reward managers for being nice to customers; (2) preface conversations with complaining customers with "We're sorry"; (3) thank the customer for bringing the problem to your attention; and (4) reward managers for solutions, not for just being nice.

I'll never get rich coming up with such simple, obvious programs. Well, maybe I'm wrong. There was *The One Minute Manager* thing. But what I know is that the adoption of the four steps I've outlined above would revolutionize customer service in this country. Perhaps it would be more accurate to say that it would institute customer service in this country. Of course, there are more elaborate approaches to customer service, and I'm not discounting them at all. I'm just saying that following my four steps would be a welcome change to the surliness, indifference, and outright rudeness that you often encounter in trying to do business with someone.

A slightly more elaborate approach, which I liked very much, used Transactional Analysis back in the 1970s. That was before TA practitioners decided they needed a universal explanation for all of human behavior—before they complicated TA beyond usefulness. In fact, American Airlines was so pleased with TA as the basis for interacting with customers that for a time they marketed their training program commercially.

Transactional Analysis was the brainchild of psychiatrist Eric Berne, who wrote a best-selling book during the 1960s, *Games People Play*. In the beginning, TA was a therapist's tool, but its simplicity soon made it very popular away from the couch. According to TA, there are three ego states in all of us: Parent, Adult, and Child. All three are legitimate and natural to the person, and people shift from one ego state to another in their transactions.

The Parent ego state is one in which we act upon transmitted knowledge, usually from parents but from other sources as well— sources such as teachers or mentors. The Parent can be nurturing: "Go ahead and cry; it will be good for you to get it out." The Parent can also be critical: "If you had listened to me, you wouldn't be in this mess."

The Child ego state is impulsive, enthusiastic, curious, and experimental. Naturalness and spontaneity characterize the Child, who is is childlike as well as childish.

The Adult reasons, gathers facts, tries to be objective, and processes data. The Adult develops options and chooses the one that seems most realistic in the situation. Anticipating the consequences of an act or a decision is a characteristic of this ego state.

The importance of TA in customer service lies in the fact that there are two kinds of transactions: complementary and crossed. In a complementary transaction, the lines of communication remain open for further exchanges. For example, the airline customer who is delayed assumes the Child and says to the passenger agent, "This is the fourth time that I've been delayed by you people. Why is it that I'm always having problems with your airline?" The passenger agent assumes the Adult: "Let me see your ticket, and perhaps we can help you. I'm sorry that you've been delayed, but perhaps we can work something out." Obviously this transaction will go further.

But in a crossed transaction, the agent might reply, "Look, we're only human. We're doing the best we can, and we deserve a little respect, too." The words may continue, but not much communication.

To an irate Child, the agent could say, "I want to do

whatever I can to help you. But first I want you to stop yelling." That's a Parent. Then the Adult takes over to deal with the facts of the situation.

Even in the treatment I've accorded TA in this brief space, you can see its possibilities in training employees to interact constructively with the public. For those of us in training, it was a marvelously straightforward, easy to understand approach to human interactions that could be taught in its basic forms in a matter of hours—very inexpensive customer service training.

Jan Carlzon of SAS, the Scandinavian airlines, justifiably has become identified with intelligent, sensitive, and responsive customer service. In 1981, he took over a money-losing airline and within a short time had turned it around by emphasizing that the assets of the airline were not its planes but its customers. He managed to communicate his vision to all SAS employees. His slogan became "If you don't serve the customer, you serve someone who does." Thus, everyone became aware that he or she was in the chain of customer service. One rather remarkable step that Carlzon took was to give great latitude and authority to anyone who dealt with customer problems and complaints. In other companies, employees had to buck the complaint or difficulty up to a supervisor, or even higher. At SAS, the person you talk to is very likely the person who will make sure something is done about your problem.

The orientation sounds simple, but in fact Carlzon, as president of SAS, has revolutionized and redesigned his company. He's getting a lot of attention these days because his vision is a rarity. And it's so sensible; that also makes it a rarity. Read his absorbing book, *Moments of Truth*.

As much as I admire what Carlzon has done, I'm hesitant to be his advocate because some people will say, "There you are. You have to do a major transformation, and we don't have the money or the time to do it." The SAS case is often presented as an exception to the rule today, but why wouldn't our wisdom dictate that Carlzon's concept of service be the rule? It seems so obvious, but apparently it isn't. If you can do a Carlzon act, you'll become a major hero, as he has. But if you adopt the Quick formula with its four steps, perhaps you'll be at least a lesser hero. You certainly will be to your customers.

Chapter 15

You Don't Know
the Truth Until
You've Heard from Others

*S*ometimes I think about being in junior philosophy again and giving Father Cronin—God rest his cantankerous, demanding soul—as bad a time as he gave me. We were all, as I recall, following the *ratio studiorum* of Saint Ignatius in a quest for reality. Now I would protest, probably either to the delight or to the horror of the venerable Jesuit priest, that my reality may not be his. Everything in old age comes under suspicion of being subjective and relative. That is ironic because presumably, as we grow older and wiser, we narrow the gap between reality and our perception of it. I've come to believe that the gap stays the same and that our awareness of it increases.

For example, I've always wondered whose perceptions of reality formed the basis of *In Search of Excellence*. I have this fantasy that Peters and Waterman interviewed top management of successful, or seemingly successful, corporations to find out what the managers thought they were doing right. Someone's perceptions were off because the stories Peters and Waterman reported about some of those corporations on their excellence list didn't quite match what I heard from people who were lower in the hierarchies of those corporations. So it wasn't a surprise for me to see that certain of those on the list later fell from grace. It just didn't seem to work out as somebody said it would.

Let me reiterate that I had a fantasy, not that I know their interviewing was selective. I don't want to get into trouble with Peters and Waterman, although with their credibility and wealth, why should they care about my imaginings? But the perceptions of people, especially of top management, present a real problem in interpreting what is and is not. Managers often assume that their perceptions of the world, and especially of their own operations, carry a special load of credibility. And after years of consulting, I'm not sure why they believe that. In fact, I get a bit weary of saying to managers who have problems with their departments or with their careers, "I know that's what you think, but what are the perceptions of others?" That they should concern themselves with how others see reality is a foreign and threatening concept to them.

I remember the embarrassment of a young supervisor having a last lunch with her boss before she departed the department for a bigger and better job. Mellowed perhaps by a glass or two of wine, her boss began to tell her how he had managed through the years. I suppose he wanted to share his wisdom and experience with her since she was advancing in managerial responsibility. He saw himself as a fair, deliberate, just person who took time to weigh all the factors in a situation before he passed judgment. He emphasized to her that one of the most important characteristics of an effective manager is predictability. As a subordinate, given the circumstances, one should be able to anticipate how the boss will act or decide. It's important, he added, that you bring your key people into the decision-making process, as he had. There's much wisdom there that a smart manager will use.

For a moment the young supervisor was torn between tact and kindness on the one hand and honesty on the other. Despite some negative feelings she had toward her soon-to-be former boss, she did respect him, and she wanted good things for him. She decided that the way he would most likely enjoy more success was to hear the truth. Drawing a deep breath, she said, "I know that you really do believe you are the way you just described yourself to me. But I think it's important to your future that you know how your subordinates see you, and it is very different from your self-image. We didn't see you as predictable. At times you came across as very autocratic and arbitrary. We felt very shut out of your decision making. True, at other times, you seemed to include us in your thinking, but then you sometimes went ahead and did what you wanted to do, even if it was contrary to what we suggested. I'm glad

I worked for you. You taught me a lot. But I have to tell you that one of the things you taught me was to manage in a way very different from you."

The moment was undoubtedly painful for him, as it was for her. And whether she accomplished anything for him, she never knew. But her predicament is not unusual. Managers often become so involved with themselves, so self-absorbed, that they are convinced their perceptions of reality are the true ones. Indeed, one of the indicators of the health of an organization is the similarity or dissimilarity between the perceptions of top management and the perceptions of employees lower in the hierarchy—once again returning to my fantasy of Peters and Waterman. My experience is that when the perceptions of top management regarding the direction and condition of the corporation are essentially the same as the perceptions of those lower in rank, the organization is a healthy one. However, when you interview top management and lower echelons and get radically different notions of what is going on, you can assume that the organization is in trouble.

One explanation for similarity of perceptions is that management has maintained open channels of communication. They have not closed themselves off from employees. They simply have assumed that we're all seeing the same things, so they work to get feedback from down below. This is the way we see it; is that the way you see it? If there is difference in perceptions, the problem may be that management simply has been stingy with information. The situation is more serious if management consciously has isolated itself from the lower echelons so as not to hear anything disturbing. Sadly, I recall one famous corporation, with excellent resources and a growing market, in which, after a change in ownership and management, the leadership imposed a wall between themselves and employees. Very little information passed in either direction, and top management seemed to be saying to employees, "There is no need for you to know what is going on. Do your job." Employees began to believe that management didn't want to know anything about the problems that employees saw. Eventually the parent company sold the troubled subsidiary, and the leadership of the new parent fired the old management, but it was too late to stop the decline. It was a needless tragedy.

Making assumptions about people, a dear friend used to preach, is one sure way to make mistakes. Managers will complain to me that people don't work the way they should, that they simply aren't motivated to do good work, that perhaps they have lost the work ethic. If I were to talk with the employees, I would almost invariably find that they had little knowledge of the nature of their managers' complaints. All they know is that they are doing a fine job and that somehow the bosses don't appreciate it.

Many managers are neglecting an essential duty of their station—communication. Periodically, a truly effective manager sits down with employees and communicates his or her goals and performance standards—the first step in managing the motivation of subordinates. Tell people what you expect them to do. Despite its obviousness, this primary step is overlooked by most managers. Why? They see no need to do it since their employees already know what is expected of them. The managers assume their employees know the goals and standards, and the employees assume they are doing what the managers want. Eventually, after big consultants' fees are paid, managers and subordinates get together and start talking.

Another step in the process of managing motivation is the one involving feedback. Here again, managers will make assumptions that employees know when they are not doing things right. When that is the case, managers tend to launch into criticism immediately, bypassing an important step—making sure the employee knows there is a problem. It's quite deflating when, after you've given an employee extensive negative feedback, he or she says, "I don't understand what you're upset about."

Employees' confusion is compounded when the manager has not set clear goals and standards. If you want to increase the chances that you will get the performance you want from employees, you must make sure that they know what you expect from them—your standards and goals—and then, before giving feedback, you must check their perceptions: "This is what we agreed on three months ago. Isn't that the way you see it?" If the employee assents, take corrective action. If the employee doesn't, then you have to find out what was unclear about your communication. The answer might well be that when your first talked about performance goals and standards, you didn't take time and care to make sure the employee understood completely what you were talking about.

In any conflict or disagreement, starting your negotiation with corrective action is a mistake because, by doing so, you may be broadcasting the message that you consider your perceptions to be an accurate reflection of reality. If you have a problem with another manager, you need to take that extra time to compare perceptions.

The term *conflict management* is a more accurate descriptor of the process than is the term *conflict resolution,* simply because the many conflicts are never completely resolved; they are just kept within manageable limits. Conflict management is most successful when the following points are kept in mind. (1) The person on the other side of the conflict has a point of view that is just as legitimate and reasonable to him or her as yours is to you. (2) The other person has the feelings and perceptions that he or she describes. The second that you seem to accuse the other person of insincerity is the second the conflict will escalate. (3) The other person is probably as un-comfortable as you are about the conflict. (4) It sometimes helps if you both express your feelings about the conflict—as well as your respective perceptions. (5) The other person is usually willing to accept a solution if you can make it sufficiently attractive. At least he or she can be persuaded to work with you to formulate a resolution of the conflict. (6) When you propose a solution, don't assume automatic acceptance by the other. You may think it is appropriate and attractive, but check the other's perception of its suitability.

Finally, much customer service will improve if we accept the customer's perceptions that they were treated discourteously or that they received shoddy material or service. Those of us in business spend too much time trying to justify ourselves when perhaps the best way to keep the customer happy is simply to say, "We're sorry that you are unhappy with us. We'd like to make you happy again because we want you to continue to do business with us."

And so, dear Father Cronin, the older I get, the more relative everything seems. It didn't seem that way in junior ontology, cosmology, and epistemology. But then, I was very young, and I, like many of my classmates, was looking for absolutes. There just aren't many of those, are there? I guess that's what your little smile suggested when we invested our time looking for certainties. No, age doesn't necessarily bring certainty or objectivity. Rather, it brings the humility to know that the way others see reality may be as important as the way we do.

Chapter 16

Handling Opposition Without Handling It

*S*everal years ago, the late Henry Ford II was arrested for driving after he'd had a few. With the auto mogul was a pretty young woman, not yet his wife. Asked by reporters about the charge and the unidentified woman, Ford said, "Never complain, never explain."

That's not bad advice. In fact, I endorse it for managers. Managers often find themselves and their ideas blocked by opposition, and when that happens, their instinct sometimes leads them to try to argue with their opponents; but this is usually not the best approach. Salespeople, who meet resistance all the time, have been trained to follow Ford's recommendations for years, and we're now beginning to understand that, for the sake of managers' effectiveness in conference rooms or in their bosses' offices, they might do well to relax instead of to rebut.

There are several reasons why we train salespeople not to respond quickly to a prospect's objection—a prospect's reason for not buying or, at least, for not buying now. The first is so the positive flow of the presentation isn't interrupted. The salesperson is, as we say, assumptive. That is, the salesperson is expecting that if he or she does a good job of matching the benefits of the product to the prospect's needs, a sale will result. The second reason the salesperson shouldn't immediately answer the opposition is so as not to reinforce the negative thoughts in the prospect's mind. You accept that the prospect has the reservation, and you go on with your presentation and your closing. Sometimes the prospect's hesitation simply disappears if you don't recognize it as important by trying to answer it.

By far the most significant reason the salesperson tries to bypass stalls or objections is that they may not be genuine. This reality is often a revelation to managers who have not been salespeople. If the prospect is not sold, he or she seizes upon the easiest explanation for not buying. A frequent objection is price: "It costs more than I want to pay," or "I don't have the money in my budget," or "Money's tight right now. See me after the first of the year." All of those responses to the selling effort may contain the same message: "I don't care what it costs. Right now, I don't see the value of your product (program, service) to me." The content of the objection may not be real, but the salesperson doesn't know for sure. So he or she will usually sidestep the objection and sell more benefits, closing again. Perhaps if the same objection reappears a couple of times, the salesperson will attempt to argue against it, suspecting that it is genuine. Had he or she jumped in to rebut it without knowing how important it was, the salesperson could have aimed artillery at ground fog.

Much the same phenomenon occurs in meetings involving managers. A manager gives a presentation to his or her bosses or to peers, pushing a project, suggestion, or idea. Someone responds, "We tried something like that in 1984, and it was a near disaster," "Those cost projections look far too optimistic. I think they need to be reworked," "This will never get past the front office now that they've ordered cutbacks," or "This is certainly admirably worked out, but there is one feature that troubles me." Objections. Stalls. They strike fear in any presenter's heart.

The usual reaction of the owner of an idea is to defend it—immediately, before the negative virus becomes serious or spreads to others. What often results is that, after the presenter has tried to show the objection or stall is not justified, the resister counters with, "But, it is justified." Now the objector is on the spot and has to come up with reasons why his or her position should be taken seriously. Others present choose sides, and, eventually, there is a vote. Sometimes there's a vote to table the idea, which is frequently a euphemism for burying it. Actually, the vote may have little to do with the intellectual content of the idea or the rationale for the project. Some people may vote because they don't like the way one side or the other conducted the debate. Or they just may get confused and say to themselves, "Let's start over some other time." In short, people's emotions probably play a role that is as important as, or perhaps more important than, their intellects.

And in the heat of it all, the presenter fails to realize that, by starting to defend the idea, he or she has lost credibility because everyone else knows the presenter has an investment in the idea. The presenter is partisan—a label that may not attach itself to the objector, who, in reality, may be just as biased for different reasons.

Salespeople understand this sequence. What I've begun to advocate is that people, such as managers, who do not see themselves as selling (although they do) receive the same training as professional salespeople. One beneficial product of the training would be discernibly less wheel spinning, time wasting, heat, and bad feelings. I now offer management trainees a five-step objection-handling sequence.

First, relax. Sit back in your chair. Keep your face impassive. Cross your legs. When you look relaxed, you not only appear confident, but you also make it easier for others to discuss your proposal openly in front of you. I once knew a manager who, at the first sign of opposition to her thinking, assumed a facial expression that was easily interpreted as, "What nonsense! How stupid these people are." She suffered a lot of stalls. No one wanted to say yes, and they were afraid to say no. So they postponed nearly everything. When you relax in the face of opposition, you disarm it. People expect to see you get red in the face, tense, maybe angry. But you don't. As salespeople say, you are assumptive.

Second, listen. When you relax, you make it easier for yourself to listen, and that's never very easy when your idea is being challenged. But you need to hear what people are saying, bad and good. The salesperson knows this is the time to get ammunition to toss back at the right moment. People in disputes usually do not listen well. They are marshaling their arguments for rebuttal. A psychologist provided me with a vivid demonstration of this in a laboratory exercise. Two teams engaged in competition by each writing a paragraph on an assigned subject. Each team selected a spokesperson to present reasons why his or her team had submitted the superior paragraph. Two judges, belonging to neither team, would pick the winner. At first, the debate between the spokespersons went quite rationally and quietly, with much good humor, but then the exchange heated up until the two were practically shouting at each other. Of course, they were being coached and egged on by their respective teams. Soon it became obvious that neither side was listening to the other. They were too busy trying to score points with the judges. Incidentally, unknown to the contestants, the judges had already secretly made their decision. The debate was staged strictly to show us how polarized and ineffective people can become when they stop listening.

Maintain eye contact with the person who is talking with you. Show that you are listening intently. The other person will usually respond to your courtesy by softening his or her comments.

Third, accept. Acceptance is not the same thing as agreement. You don't buy the substance of the opposition, but you do acknowledge that the other person feels the way he or she says. Giving acceptance is being respectful of the other. None of us likes to have our feelings or our intelligence discounted in any way. We do not like hearing the suggestion that we are silly or wrong or that we have no right to believe the way we do. Therefore, an important factor in winning people over is to recognize and accept their opinions and feelings.

A fascinating phenomenon sometimes occurs at this point. Since you don't argue or say much of anything, the prospect may feel a need to elaborate. He or she may do so to such an extent that the person finally says, "Maybe it isn't as important as it seemed at first."

Fourth, move on. Sell some more benefits. Don't rebut. Don't say, "Yes, I understand why you might feel that way, but if you look at the cost projections you'll see . . ." No matter how tactfully or elegantly you put it, you're saying, "Yes, I hear you, I understand what you're saying, but you're wrong." It is almost universal that people do not wish to hear they are wrong. It follows therefore that you do not accomplish much for yourself by saying someone who opposes you is wrong, so you sidestep the objection. You don't ignore it; you've already accepted that the person believes or feels the way he or she does. You use a "Yes, and . . ." response instead of a "Yes, but . . ." "Yes, I understand that the cost projections are a consideration, and here's something else I'd like you to consider." Follow that with another benefit. If the objection about the cost projections keeps coming up, then go to the last step.

Fifth, qualify the objection and answer briefly. Now you're ready to confirm that the resistance is genuine. Restate the objection as you've heard it, get the other's agreement that you have stated it accurately, then say, "If I could demonstrate that the cost projections are realistic rather than optimistic, would you be in favor of the plan?" If the objector replies, "Yes," then prove your point. If, however, the objector replies, "I don't know that," then you have a hidden objection that you may want to dig out. One way, of course, is to say, "I'm prepared to show you that the cost figures are reasonable. But I think you have some other concerns, and it would be helpful if you told me what they are."

Throughout the entire five steps, your most potent tool is silence. Most people talk too much. Silence not only enables you to listen, it puts pressure on the other person to talk. People feel tense when silence prevails. That tension works for you. Make your point and fall silent. The other person will feel that he or she is expected to say something. You can never hear too much. The more others talk, the more ammunition you'll get to come back and sell harder.

Silence is especially effective in a group situation. If you take your time responding, or show no inclination to respond at all, someone else in the room may do it for you. And if they are not identified with the proposal, they have more credibility and weight than you. Whenever I'm in a selling mode in a group, I try to make my issue a group issue. A few years ago, I sat on a board of directors in which I frequently met opposition to my ideas from a very articulate woman. At one session, when my antagonist was not present, the board acted favorably on a proposal of mine. During the next meeting, she reacted vehemently to my idea, chastising me for having presented it. I sat and listened. She kept talking, probably because I wouldn't respond. Finally, another board member broke in, obviously exasperated, and said, "Look, Betty, it was Tom's idea, but we discussed it thoroughly and voted on it. We'll be glad to tell you about our discussion, but we won't undo the vote." Betty fell silent. My case had been fought for me.

Both as a salesman and as a consultant working in group dynamics, I've found lots of reasons to go against the fighting instinct and practice Henry Ford's advice. When I don't complain, when I don't explain any more than I have to, I often put the pressure on others to do the work for me. And they often do the work remarkably well.

Chapter 17

Sensitivity Goes with Power

believe I've come up with one of the best paradoxes since G. K. Chesterton used to make them up over breakfast. "How many of you," I ask my audiences, "believe that powerful people are sensitive people?" There are usually not many believers. "Well," I say, "truly powerful people are some of the most sensitive people in the world."

For most in the audience, it's a startling contradiction in terms. The powerful people they've known haven't appeared sensitive. But the reason their perceptions and mine differ is that they are using a narrow definition of sensitivity. Webster's dictionary defines it as "awareness of the needs and emotions of others." Being aware of the needs of others is not the same as being affected by them, and sensitivity is not always the same as sympathy and compassion. There are some who consider sensitivity to be a wimpy trait. But powerful people are not wimpy.

Margaret V. Higginson and I, some years back, wrote an article, "Sensitivity—The Missing Ingredient for Success," for a business periodical. (Apparently the subject was startling to the editors. They didn't publish it for two years and then only at the back of the magazine.) We acknowledged that the idea might be a bit strange when talking about fast-track, powerful people and that the trait of sensitivity seems at odds with the other admired characteristics of high-powered people—characteristics such as aggressiveness and competitiveness. But we focused, in that article, on describing the differences among sensitivity, insensitivity, and hypersensitivity.

Sensitivity. Sensitive people operate as open systems, interacting in healthy ways with people and organizations. They are centered as opposed to self-centered and can respond to others without losing a sense of what and where they are. They can accord space to others as required. Sensitive people have boundaries that are firm but permeable. They take feedback from others, with some caution, stopping to consider whether the feedback is well-founded.

Insensitivity. Insensitive people are self-centered and have problems concerning themselves with others, even when those others can benefit them, their career, their power, and their influence. They erect high psychological barriers that protect them from the perceptions and feedback of others. They avoid anything that might threaten their self-images.

Hypersensitivity. While the self-centered person rejects feedback that is at variance with his or her self-image, the hypersensitive person may have extreme reactions to any shortcomings or faults. They have inadequate boundaries that fail to protect them from external influences.

Building and keeping power are a matter of forging alliances with others, of tradeoffs, of looking for opportunities and seizing them before others do, and of being considered crucial to others— especially to bosses. You must have a sense of what others— especially powerful others—want and need and a sense of what you can supply them to make yourself more important.

Excessively self-centered and hypersensitive people have trouble staying on the power track. The former miss the signs of change and the negative feelings others have toward them. The latter see the signs but fail to analyze them before reacting defensively. Neither is sufficiently rooted in reality to know what is happening around them and to them. These are the people who often find themselves bypassed for promotions or terminated. And whatever their fate, it usually comes as a nasty surprise to them. There was a story recently in the business press that reinforces this truth. The CEO of a very large corporation had apparently been drawing apart from his board—or vice versa—for more than a year. He went into the quarterly board meeting expecting to be congratulated and supported, but he was fired instead. It was news to him.

Through all of your alliances and shifting loyalties, you cannot afford to lose your identity. In fact, if people are to trust you (and trust plays a big role in power relationships), they must have a sense that you know who you are. Otherwise they will not work comfortably with you. And they may even scheme to take some of your power away from you. You must know how people regard you. By being able to encourage, receive, and evaluate feedback from others, you cannot only help yourself get in better touch with your feelings, but you can also win the respect and confidence of others. They will come to you and work with you because you are self-confident, open, and trustworthy.

Years ago, sociologist Alfred McClung Lee, in a book entitled *Multivalent Man,* described the person who can relate to different people with different values, from different cultures, and in different contexts. The relationship is not built on sympathy or necessarily on any close emotional identification. Rather, it is built on an openness to others' opinions, wants, and needs—on sensing where others might be. His profile resembles that of Michael Maccoby's gamesman, described in the best-selling book of that name—*The Gamesman.* Maccoby presented the gamesman as a person who, in his research, proved to be the most influential type of manager. The label that Maccoby used is an unfortunate one because people who are seen as playing games are suspected and looked down upon. The gamesman and the multivalent man are able to recognize that many of their contacts with other people are transactions in which all parties hope to gain something.

Even in conversations among co-workers, there are usually agendas. Each person has his or her purpose or objective. People who are successful in building and maintaining power (and *maintaining* is a word equal in value to *building*) make themselves aware of what is going on in a transaction. Each person brings certain attitudes, patterns of behavior, preferences, and prejudices to the transaction. The sensitive person sees a need to ask, "What's going on right now? Why is the other person acting this way? Am I achieving what I want to achieve?"

Sensitive people become good listeners for two reasons. First, they listen to determine their effectiveness with others and second, they listen to find out what the other person wants. They learn to detect those small signals others send out regarding feelings, needs, and wants, and they learn to detect reactions to what is being said and done. Sensitive people ask one of the most important questions of all: "Does what is going on now enhance or detract from our getting what we both want?" People on the power track, not surprisingly, are strongly goal oriented. It's characteristic of influential people that they know what they want and believe they have every right to try to get it.

An English foreign minister of the last century said, "Great Britain has no friends, only interests." Very often, powerful people come across that way. They make friends and relationships pragmatically. But sensitivity on a one-to-one basis is not enough. People on the power track must be tuned in to events in their work groups and larger organizations of which they are a part. Changes in the environment can alter work relationships and can influence, as well as threaten, authority and competence. The power person needs to be sensitive and objective as well as tough because he or she must be aware of what's happening and what changes—economic, organizational, and political (inside and out)—threaten his or her position and require adjustments, some of which may be painful.

In one company I knew, the president was insensitive, but his executive vice president was hypersensitive. The president managed to isolate himself from key people in the organization who had essential information about the products and competition. Even his office was tucked away in a corner of the building with an entrance that looked as if it had been built to withstand siege. His physical and psychological boundaries precluded any reception of information relating to how the company was running.

His vice president had virtually no boundaries at all. He was such a totally open system that he had almost no identity of his own. He constantly molded himself into a shape that he felt was pleasing to the person he wanted to interact with. He made no permanent impression, and it is likely that no one made a permanent impression on him.

The two of them had ascended to power in a company that had fifty years of growth and success behind it. Within a few years they drove that company into the ground.

Even the most powerful and politically astute people can lose their way temporarily. In this century, Franklin D. Roosevelt was probably the most powerful American president. Yet, for a moment, he forgot that his power was built largely on his understanding of his constituents. He decided, much against the advice of those around them, that the Supreme Court needed to be taught a lesson and neutralized because the justices had declared some of his New Deal legislation unconstitutional. He backed a plan to expand the Court with new appointees who, presumably, would be more agreeable to FDR's wishes. FDR became insensitive to what the people wanted from him. They did not want the Supreme Court packed. As a result, FDR suffered a resounding defeat and probably never quite recovered the power and esteem he had enjoyed before the incident.

If you want to see truly sensitive people in action, watch skillful salespeople. They are pragmatic. In most cases, they are not interested in building friendships, but they are involved in building relationships based in large part on their knowing the needs and wants of their customers and then supplying them.

But I guess that's another stereotype shot to blazes. Most people don't identify salespeople with sensitivity.

Chapter 18

Training Is Too Important to Be Left to Trainers

*T*he training field represents a sad paradox. On the one hand, there is no field that is more vital than training to the interests of American business today. On the other, many training practitioners are ill-equipped to serve those interests.

Quite simply, in our global economy, the United States is too often undersold and outproduced, quantitatively and qualitatively. We used to think that American management know-how put us far ahead of the rest of the world—and it probably did. But, unfortunately, we didn't have a corner on good management, although we Americans find it hard to accept that reality.

While much of the research in the behavioral sciences, particularly about employee productivity, was accomplished in this country, our own managements tended to pay little attention to it. But European and Asian managements were hungry for it, and they applied that research and the basic concepts that flowed from it. Meanwhile, American managements sponsored training, or at least tolerated it, without assuming responsibility for making sure that it produced the results that were needed—qualified supervisors and managers who knew how to get the most from their people. Training was considered a cost center, and that was quite all right because American corporations were making money despite what they did.

The training profession should offer leadership, or at least guidance, to American business managements to help them cope with the challenges of the international market. But most practitioners in the field never intended training to be their profession; it is a second career for most. There is little academic career preparation, and there is no credentialing. The field is unique, unfortunately, in that today, you can be a schoolteacher in transition; tomorrow, in an entry-level training position, you can call yourself a trainer; and on the third day, according to one cynical veteran, you can call yourself a consultant.

An exaggeration? Somewhat. But the reality is that both managements and trainers exist in an uneasy, ill-defined relationship—a situation detrimental to both. The recent history is that management often expects trainers to take the initiative in suggesting and designing programs that will equip managers to deal with the new challenges. Trainers, however, traditionally have seen themselves in a reactive staff role, taking directions from management.

The problem has even deeper roots. Management often displays a fix-it mentality. If you have a problem, go find someone who can fix it. But training and developing a work force to be and to stay effective is not like calling in a plumber or even a computer expert. Nevertheless, trainers have become accustomed to fixing it— bringing in some kind of program that will ostensibly meet the need or relieve the pressure. Consequently, in many organizations, neither management nor trainers take responsibility for the long-term results of training.

Management and trainers often share a quaint and old-fashioned view of learning as taking place only in a classroom. The concept of continuing development is not one that you'll find often. Management sees their responsibility as paying for the classroom and rounding up the people to sit in it. Trainers, most of whom have come from a teaching background, see their obligation as one of coming up with a curriculum and conducting classes, as most of them did with youngsters. What actually goes on in the corporate classroom may have little or no resemblance to what occurs on the work scene, and the content of the classes may not be in sync with the organizational culture. If there is such a dichotomy between the classroom and the workplace, not only will the learning be invalidated, but there may also be a side effect of cynicism. Future training will be seen as another time-consuming and useless venture.

The deficiencies I've pointed out in the training and development of our business leaders will continue to plague us, to drain away our money, and to build resistance to learning unless management and trainers join in making three important changes in the way they view training and the roles of trainers.

First, Trainers Must See Themselves as Helping to Run the Business. Very often, the training director runs the training department. I'm sure that such compartmentalization exists throughout many corporations, but trainers have—or should have—an impact on the corporation for years into the future. Their parochialism can seriously impede a corporations's growth and effectiveness.

In many speeches I've given to training professionals, I've taken a verbal survey to determine how many in the audience see themselves as business people. I ask them to raise their hands to show me how many regularly read publications such as the *Wall Street Journal, Business Week, Fortune,* and the like. In the average training audience, few hands go up. (I should add that many of the trainers present admit they don't read publications relating to the training profession either.)

One of the examples I cite is that of a woman who joined a bank as a trainer. She used the tuition refund program to get her MBA degree in finance, and she used another employer reimbursement plan to earn a certificate in financial planning. Later, she joined a Wall Street firm and took the Series Seven to entitle her to a broker's license, even though she had no intention of selling. That's the kind of total commitment to the business that trainers should make and that management should encourage and reward.

Second, Trainers Must Get Out of the Classroom. Because of our traditional view of learning as taking place in a classroom, we have been slow to realize that our business organizations are learning laboratories. Learning is going on at all times and in all places. But is it what management wants? Will such learning contribute to the well-being of the corporation? In some progressive organizations, trainers are expected to act as consultants, helping their internal clients to identify problems, needs, and opportunities. Then the trainers design programs to solve the problems, meet the needs, and take advantage of the opportunities. This active kind of role for

trainers is in contrast to the catalogue kind of operation in which
the training department pushes out its product line irrespective of
the wants and needs of the market. In marketing terms, using
trainers in the dual roles of consulting and training results more
nearly in a push-pull effort, or, in more contemporary terms, in a
market-driven operation.

Of course, when trainers get out of the classoom, they are
exposed to the language, concerns, and realities of their prospective
clients. And to function as consultants, they must learn the
operation. Both trainer and client benefit because the trainer brings
an objective, third-party perspective and becomes integrated into
the business.

Third, Trainers and Management Must Emphasize Results.
Surprisingly, a large number of managements and trainers evaluate
inputs rather than outputs. Appraisal systems judge performance
on efficient activity—for example, an employee takes initiative,
works well with others, is loyal, enthusiastic, and mature. These are
all important, of course, but they may have nothing to do with what
happens as a result of their application. Trainers are fond of talking
about how many courses and workshops are available in their
catalogues, how many trainees they have run through a particular
program, how modern their training facilities are, and so on.
Ironically, the measurement of success is how many people have
been through a two-day seminar on delegation rather than how
many managers have saved how much time by delegating some of
their tasks to subordinates.

Trainers, unfortunately, have traditionally been accused of
emphasizing form over content. Of the three components of adult
learning—content, methodology, and process—methodology has
been seen as the primary concern of trainers. The implication is that
how something is delivered is more important than what is
delivered, and there seems to be some truth to this. I've sat through
many dismal presentations that were loaded with ideas but that,
nevertheless, received very low ratings from trainers. Conversely,
I've been present for flashy, entertaining sessions that were skimpy
on content, but the ratings went through the ceiling. The third
component of adult learning is the process—what goes on between

people. Process is an area vital to the success of training but one in which even many trainers have not been trained.

How do my three "musts" translate efficiency into effectiveness based on results? The most important consideration is that training is a shared responsibility. The manager supposedly knows his or her people better than anyone else. The manager also should be the person most aware of immediate needs—what the department will require in the way of skills and knowledge in the forseeable future. In the early days of training and organization development, line managers were frequently asked to step out of the line into training positions. The assumption was that not only did these people understand the needs of management, they also had more credibility when presenting training proposals to their colleagues. But despite their knowledge of the organization and, in many cases, despite their zeal, they sometimes lacked training and consulting skills.

In an ideal situation, the manager consults with the training specialist or is consulted by him or her. The trainer should be locked into some sort of strategic or operating plan and should be able to say to the manager, "Here's what your people will need." In some organizations there is an advisory group made up of members of functional groups, administrators, and trainers. These people, plugged into the planning, make assessments of the needs of the organization and plan the training accordingly. The advisory group should have a mandate from the top, such as the one a training director told me of recently: Create a competitive work force.

When trainers enter departments, they should form partnerships with the managers to determine the training needs: Who needs what skills? Then the means of training is decided. Shall it be classroom or on the job? We do not take sufficient advantage of learning at work. Shall it be theoretical as well as experiential? Remember that the closer the learning is to the actual work situation, the more durable will be the retention of the knowledge. What will happen as a result of the learning? Here is what exists now. What will the new department look like after people have acquired the skills and the knowledge that will come with the training? This is the behavior we see now; what will the behavior be then? How will we know the training has been a success?

Training isn't an academic issue. It isn't something that would be nice to do or something that, perhaps, we should have. Training is what people decide they must have for the sake of people's capability and the continuing effectiveness of the organization. Training is or should be an investment that leads to greater effectiveness and to a reasonable return on the investment. It is not a cost center that is tolerable within certain limits.

The frequently observed dichotomy between the functional departments and the training departments must give way to a partnership in which training is dominated neither by the human resources people nor by the functional people. Trainers and managers play consultative and collaborative roles for each other, and trainers can no longer focus only on running training departments, as they often have. Instead, trainers must join forces with functional managers, not only in running the business more effectively but also in developing its human assets to meet the challenges of the future.

Part Four

KNOWING WHAT'S REALLY HAPPENING IN YOUR ORGANIZATION

*f*inally, there is your relationship to your organization. You can hardly be effective without seeing clearly what is happening in your environment. There are many bits of so-called conventional wisdom that can clutter up your scene and keep you from really understanding the world in which you work. For example, take the idea that managing is soft stuff, as opposed to the hard matter of technology. In fact, we have done our theoretical homework. We know a lot about how human beings behave on the work scene. We know much about what employees respond to favorably— and much about what they don't. We've actually moved far beyond the theories and the concepts. Many of us are well aware from experience what works and what doesn't.

We gained some of that experience through espousing a few of the fads and movements through the years, but even many of the movements and techniques and programs that we've disdained as fads have left some essential knowledge with us.

In this section, you'll find that many of the emphases you're familiar with in your organization have been misplaced through the years. Much of management development doesn't develop; it's wasted time and effort. Power is often a dirty word, yet just try to build your career and effectiveness without it. Managers concentrate on employees' morale, which may have no essential relationship to how those employees work. And complexity doesn't always indicate higher truths.

We're fond of these traditional biases, which have been handed down from generation to generation. But it's time to take an unconventional view of them.

Chapter 19

There's No Soft Stuff in Managing

*T*here's an irony in the title of Milan Kundera's novel, *The Unbearable Lightness of Being:* When people fill their being, it usually isn't light. It can get very heavy. Much the same kind of thing can be said about the so-called softness of managing: It can become very hard. I realize that the word *hard* is ambiguous. It can mean difficult, or it can mean firm. Both are true. But most people who manage acknowledge that managing is difficult, but its firmness as a discipline is, in their minds, open to question.

In fact, it has become quite fashionable to refer to management development and training as soft stuff. Recently, a CEO of a large corporation announced a new development program for its managers, but the tone was unmistakably tentative. They were going to try it, he said, but he added that everyone knew that such training was soft and therefore might not take. Still, they would experiment.

What drivel, I thought. For years, I've been preaching, confidently, that we know almost everything we have to know about how to manage people successfully—that is, how to get people to commit themselves to organizational goals and to work effectively and productively to achieve them. And what we know, or should know, is very hard knowledge. Perhaps I've done many managers an injustice when, in moments of pique, I have suggested that they continue to pretend we don't have a knowledge base for managing. It's possible, after all, that they really don't know, in which case, we in human resources have done a less than admirable job in incorporating years of credible research into our training base. We should have contradicted the traditional perspective that management is soft stuff. It is as hard as hard can be.

I sometimes feel that many managers—and trainers—believe that management research had its genesis in the 1960s, when Maslow, McGregor, and Herzberg became celebrities. Certainly, McGregor's Theory Y assumptions about people attracted a lot of attention as he described employees who find work to be as natural as rest—employees who commit themselves to objectives they find valuable and who not only accept but seek responsibility.

But seeds of our modern thinking were present in the Hawthorne studies, conducted in the late 1920s and early 1930s. Researchers found that giving employees some control over their own work had a positive impact on productivity. These were the people who not only accepted responsibility but welcomed it—and increased their output accordingly. Furthermore, the success of many companies that adopted the Scanlon Plan, introduced in 1938, should have convinced all of us long ago that people who are given a stake in the improvement of their operation respond imaginatively, just as McGregor noted: "The capacity to exercise a relatively high degree of imagination, ingenuity, and creativity in the solution of organization problems is widely, not narrowly, distributed in the population." So successful has employee imagination been in some companies using the Scanlon Plan that their managements won't talk about the details because those results have given them competitive advantages.

Abraham Maslow, with his hierarchy of needs, was instrumental in persuading us to think about people's requirements for living. Not only did Maslow awaken us to the needs of people at work, but he also discovered the reality that people have differing needs at different times. When Maslow published his famous book, *Motivation and Personality,* in the 1950s, thinking about people's needs was much simpler and rather uniform, as I can testify, because that's when I started my career. It was generally assumed that most people in corporate America were working to earn money that would buy them the material things they wanted—a house, a car, nice vacations, and college for the kids. There were some who also wanted advancement, status, prestige, But for most, the personal objective was money. Or that's what management thought.

That assumption is the reason my own restlessness early in my career befuddled my bosses. I enjoyed a job that gave me the partial autonomy of a field office with the backing of a large, prestigious corporation. I was virtually guaranteed more money each year because I earned not only a salary but also commissions on the business produced in my region. But after about five years, when I was making good money, I asked, "Okay, what's next?" I was bored doing the same things. Regardless of the money, I couldn't see myself staying put. That kind of search for rewards other than money was somewhat new to the management of the day.

While Maslow was a seminal thinker, his theory of motivation, which incorporated the hierarchy, was not successfully demonstrated in lab research. So we can't really say that his was hard knowledge. Much more firm was the research of Rensis Likert, who was at one time director of the Institute for Social Research at the University of Michigan. For years Likert conducted surveys to discover what managers themselves regarded as the environment most conducive to optimum productivity. Likert defined four organizational profiles: System 1—exploitative authoritative; System 2—benevolent authoritative; System 3—consultative; System 4—participative group. Managers surveyed indicated that they believed the closer their organizations moved toward System 4, the more productive and effective they were in accomplishing their goals.

A System 4 organization is characterized by management's trust in employees and vice versa. People are motivated by rewards. There is relatively free communication—up, down, and sideways. People at all levels get involved in making decisions on issues that affect them and in which they have expertise. Likert developed an instrument of measurement, named after him, that showed that after a program of organizational change in which effectiveness was increased throughout the system the employees perceived the organization to have moved from being System 1 or System 2 to being somewhere between Systems 3 and 4.

In 1961, he published his work in *New Patterns of Management.* I don't recall that it received much attention here in the United States, but many of the principles involved in Likert's work went to Japan, where they were eagerly and successfully adapted to that more collegial society. We've all seen the results. Ironically, William Ouchi would enjoy a best-selling book, in the 1980s,

Theory Z, that reported on a so-called miracle that had been based, in part, on the principles of participative management.

As the Japanese have proved, Likert's work is pretty hard stuff. Certainly the Japanese have made it work. And some American companies that have moved toward the participative styles of management have had good results. That's undoubtedly an understatement. Almost every expert in management sees American business as moving inexorably toward a more open, participative atmosphere because, by 1989, we all knew what Likert knew more than thirty years ago: People tend to work best in an environment that gives them more control over their work and lives. We should have realized that after the publication of *Management and the Worker* way back in 1939, which described the Hawthorne research by two people who were there: Fritz J. Roethlisberger and William J. Dickson.

Much more influential than Likert has been B. F. Skinner, the brilliant Harvard psychologist. Although derided by many other psychologists for his so-called rat psychology (actually, Skinner used pigeons), his work not only is sound, but it offers the potential for changing our organizations to achieve what I believe could be the highest productivity ever experienced. The essence of Skinner's operant conditioning or positive reinforcement is that the behavior you want in others can be shaped through rewards. Just as Skinner conditioned the behavior of pigeons in the lab by teaching them how to peck on levers to get food, managers can change the behavior of people who work for them by giving them rewards. You can see where the derision entered in: People are not pigeons pecking for food.

But the principles of positive reinforcement are valid for people too. Behavior that is reinforced (rewarded) tends to be repeated if the reward is valuable to the doer. The difference between pigeons and people is that no one tells pigeons what is gong on, whereas it's quite acceptable, even desirable, to tell people what's going on. "We're going to reward the behavior we want; we won't reward the behavior we don't want." Obvious? No, it doesn't seem to be, judging by the practice of most managements, which reward all sorts of things, such as longevity, loyalty, good manners, and attendance—things that may have little or nothing to do with productivity.

Using Skinnerian principles, the manager makes it clear what he or she wants in terms of employee behavior—usually by explaining the manager's goals as well as standards of performance. While the employee works at doing what the manager wants, the manager gives feedback—negative when the performance isn't according to standards, positive when it is. When the employee is successful, the manager finds a way to reward the accomplishment, either by more praise or some monetary or other nonmonetary recognition. Once the behavior has been shaped, the manager takes care to help the employee maintain it by intermittent reinforcement. For example, the manager might say, "I want you to know how much I appreciate your having reached the level of 98 percent accuracy and staying there." Behavior that has been shaped and rewarded need be recognized only at intervals to be maintained.

The lab results with pigeons are there for everyone to see. The organizational results with people are also quite apparent when managers have consistently and conscientiously practiced positive reinforcement. There's nothing manipulative or deceptive about it when the employee is clear about the manager's expectations. And whispers about brainwashing are totally off the point. In the ideal manager-subordinate relationship, both are clear and aboveboard about the behavior the manager wants. In such a relationship, there's no need or room for deceptive practices. And if they are once employed, there will be no future openness because there will be no trust.

Motivation to achieve rewards is essential to operant conditioning, and it is part of classic motivation theory, which some managers seem to regard as the softest stuff of all. Expectancy Theory, about which I've written often, is mainstream psychology. It is simple to understand and easy to apply. People don't doubt its validity; they just don't know it. Frederick Herzberg's work is much more well-known and popular. In the thirty years or so since it was published, it has acquired tremendous validity. People simply accept that employees are motivated by work, by achievement, by recognition of achievement, by responsibility, by advancement, and by possibility for growth. One of the practical applications of the theory has been job enrichment, which was pioneered by Robert Ford at AT&T and M. Scott Myers at Texas Instruments. The idea of enriching people's work by pushing down responsibility from a higher level has become irreversibly established.

Turning from individuals to groups, we have volumes and volumes of data from the 1950s through the 1970s—the most intense years for research on people in small groups—to show us how people can be effective in collaborative situations. Such research has been invaluable in training people how to run meetings, how to build teams, and how to create employee involvement programs. The empirical data collected by psychologists as well as by management in the past decades provide indisputable evidence demonstrating how people in groups work effectively.

Finally, adult learning theory has shown us how adults learn. Adults must have a reason for learning—a reason that provides value for them, and they must be able to apply what they've learned. During application, they need feedback to help fix the learning and to correct the application. And last, they need to be rewarded for having successfully learned and applied. Yet, we still train adults the old-fashioned way. We bring them to a classroom; we provide no compelling rationale for the learning; we create an artificial environment that may resemble the work scene only incidentally; we return the trainee to the same old problems; and we pay little or no attention to whether learning has taken place. As one educator said to me, "We take the fish out of the polluted lake, clean him up, and throw him back into the dirty lake."

We know better. We have decades of research and application and validation behind us. We know what we need to know to get positive responses from employees—to raise productivity and commitment. Yet, we treat it all as if we were nailing gelatin to the wall. It is all, we say, soft stuff.

No. The facts show that it is very hard stuff. It is firm. It is difficult. Maybe it's just unbearably difficult.

Chapter 20

Some Fads Have
an Enduring Legacy

*O*ne of the more predictable recurring fads in management is the disdain of all fads. The so-called New Age training has brought it around again. The trigger for the disdain is the disillusionment that comes from some new supposed panacea that isn't—as nothing is—a cure for everything. The word *fad* itself has a pejorative connotation. Webster's dictionary defines the word as "a practice or interest followed for a time with exaggerated zeal." Well, I've seen a lot of exaggerated zeal in my time, so you can imagine that I've seen a lot of fads and fad bashing. *Business Week* did quite a job a couple of years ago on the Managerial Grid, Managing by Objectives (MBO), and Theory Z. My first reaction to fad bashing is, "Right on," probably because I've never produced a fad. Envy? Absolutely. Who would turn up his or her nose at having one's book sell one or two million copies? That would mean you could always fly first class.

But hold on. Some so-called fads have changed the way we think about managing, even if they are no longer popular in their original form. Take the Grid, developed by Robert R. Blake and the late Jane S. Mouton. Although the eminent German-American psychologist Kurt Lewin had defined three styles of managing—authoritarian, democratic, and laissez-faire—Blake and Mouton provided much more specificity. Terms such as *9.1 management* or *5.5 management* became part of everyday talk for some. Through self-examination and the feedback of others, you could plot your own style of managing. In one corner of the Grid was the task-oriented manager whose concern for people was low. In another corner was the opposite: the so-called country club manager, whose concern for people was high, but his or her results might not be.

The classification that nearly everyone sought was in the 9.9 corner: "Work accomplishment is from committed people; interdependence through a 'common stake' in organization purpose leads to relationships of trust and respect." In 9.9 management, the old dichotomy between task orientation and people orientation disappeared. You realized that you could get the best results if you gave equal concern to the tasks and to the people performing them.

If such a conclusion seems obvious today, that's because the Grid influence was so pervasive. Grid seminars attracted thousands and thousands of managers, many of whom, for the first time, received feedback from other managers about their styles of managing. Although, in the self-evaluations that preceded the seminar, many managers saw themselves as 9.9, the actual feedback during the seminars showed that the majority were far more task-oriented than concerned for people. It's fair to say that the Grid popularized the notion that it is appropriate and profitable to show interest in the well-being of employees.

To judge the enormous impact of this relationship, you have to understand the atmosphere that existed in most businesses in the 1950s and early 1960s. Prevailing management style was paternalistic and, to use the definition of Rensis Likert, benevolent authoritative. Likert, a distinguished social scientist, described such an organization thus: "Management and employees exist in a master-servant relationship. Communication is mostly down from above. There is limited involvement of employees in setting goals or participation in decision making. It's not an unfriendly system but there isn't much latitude given to employees to do their thing."

Self-actualization, a term introduced by Abraham Maslow in the 1950s, means becoming what you are capable of being—self-fulfillment. Self-actualization was a growth need most people did not expect to satisfy working in an organization in the 1950s. But today, we take it for granted that self-actualization is a need everyone is entitled to work to meet if he or she desires.

Likert's ground-breaking work in participative management went relatively unrecognized for a long time in the United States. His research purported to show that the organization most effective in reaching its goals is System 4—group participative. It very closely resembles the definition that Blake and Mouton gave to 9.9 management, cited earlier. There is high involvement by employees in setting and achieving organizational goals. Communication is vertical and horizontal. A high level of trust exists between management and employees. Unfortunately, System 4 did not become a fad in the United States, but many of Likert's principles found fertile ground in Japan. They would come back to us years later in William Ouchi's best-selling book *Theory Z*.

Members of a group giving feedback to other members was something quite new in the 1960s when Blake and Mouton designed it into their seminars. But they weren't the first. Sensitivity training was already becoming popular. Kurt Lewin had stumbled onto that idea back in 1946 when he and his colleagues were consultants to a group of teachers meeting in Connecticut. Lewin, who was studying the dynamics of people in small groups, met each night with his associates to discuss what they had seen in the groups in which they sat. One of the teachers asked to sit in on the postmortem and received feedback on her participation that day. More teachers asked to join the discussion groups in the evening, and the idea to give feedback to the members of groups on their effectiveness was born.

By the late 1960s, sensitivity training was attracting all kinds of people—not only professionals, trainers, and educators but people from all walks of life. In fact, the group movement was surging forward. Suddenly we became aware of T (for training) groups, encounter groups, marathons, and so on. Many were unstructured, that is, led or facilitated by people who were not qualified, and they probably resembled group therapy in some cases. A few companies experimented with groups as part of their training, but many employees found the intimacy of such groups to be very stressful. People often discovered much more about their co-workers than they cared to know.

The relative lack of structure gave way to what was then called the instrumented lab. Quite simply, such groups controlled what went on through the use of instruments—self-evaluations, forms that channeled the feedback, and measuring devices for gauging effectiveness of the group. The value of the instrumented group was that it provided an atmosphere in which people could learn through feedback without exposing themselves to hurtful comments by those who often used sensitivity training as an outlet for their aggressions or as an opportunity to get some cheap therapy.

The instrumented lab, of which the Grid seminar was an example, offered at least two substantial benefits for those of us practicing in management effectiveness today. First, the continuing research into the behavior of people in small groups provided invaluable guidance in how to achieve better problem solving and decision making, and second, many of the techniques used in instrumented groups are now being applied regularly in team building in work groups.

A good illustration of the instrumented lab was Robert B. Morton's Organization Development Lab. Phase 1 was very much devoted to training. Participants in groups of eight or ten would take part in various simulated exercises. After each, the participants would evaluate their own effectiveness and that of the whole group in completing the tasks. Toward the end of the one-week lab, each participant would use a feedback form to tell every other participant how he or she judged that person's effectiveness in the group's activities—in introducing ideas or supporting those of others, in being open and honest, in working to resolve conflict, and so on. Of course, negative activities, such as dominating or seeking too much recognition, were also judged.

Phase 1 of the lab could be a stranger group—people who didn't work in the same company—or a cousin lab—people who worked with the same organization but didn't usually work together—or a family—people who interacted on a regular basis. Phase 2 usually brought together people who worked in proximity and who sometimes depended on one another to get the work done. This time the content was a real problem that existed on the work scene. Participants used their collaborative and feedback skills from the first lab to help them work through to a solution.

While the so-called era of the group has faded, we still use the theories and techniques developed during its heyday. Anyone engaging in team building owes a debt to the pioneers like Morton, Blake, and Mouton. We now have terms such as *group process*— what goes on between people in a group, that is, the dynamics—and the *facilitator*—the person who aids, nudges, and guides (but does not lead) the group toward its objectives.

Speaking of objectives, managing by objectives (MBO) became a buzzword during the 1960s. The idea that managers would sit down with employees on a periodic basis and enlist their aid in achieving certain formal goals was a practice first advocated by Peter Drucker and subsequently promoted by George Odiorne, a professor at the University of Michigan. It's a simple idea whose purpose is to move everyone in an organization in the same direction. And it's quite consistent with the trend to greater involvement, in that some of the goals can be negotiated between managers and their subordinates.

It is mystifying that MBO has not been the pervasive success it should have been. Both Maslow and McGregor, the latter famous for his Theory X and Theory Y, pointed out that goals were natural to human behavior. People need reasons for what they do, and if the goals of an organization make sense to them, and if they help to achieve some of their personal goals, people will commit themselves to those organizational goals. Thus, MBO seems like a natural. But if you look at the appraisal systems of most organizations, you'll see they are not based on MBO. People generally are not evaluated on how well they achieve the agreed-upon goals.

Probably one of the reasons MBO has not swept the business community is that it takes rigorous commitment for several years before it becomes an accepted way of doing things. Once goals have been established, they must be monitored and evaluated at the end of the period for which they've been set. If managers start getting careless, if they overlook or "forgive" goals that are not reached, or if they don't evaluate people's performance on the basis of the goals, then the system will wither.

However, there's no question about the impact of the MBO movement and Odiorne's evangelism: setting goals is commonplace. But, unfortunately, goal setting is not the essence of good management; it often seems to be an adjunct activity.

Looking back over the past thirty years at the impact of people such as Maslow, McGregor, Blake and Mouton, Likert, Odiorne, Lewin, and others associated with group research, we've seen a lot of currents. Some people call them fads. Even so, they are not fluff. And they've had a permanent impact on the way managers think and act. As we move—and we are moving—toward more participative organizational environments, as we strive to build more effective work groups, and as we continually define the profiles of managerial behavior that gets results, we have to acknowledge that what many have called fads have become values that are permanently a part of our heritage.

Perhaps the only fad we should reject out of hand is the automatic looking down on fads.

Chapter 21

Upgrading Permanent
to Temporary

*T*he spring of 1968 was aha! time for me, a season for a
new truth. I was still sorting out the meaning of a significant
experience I'd had with a task force when a speech by Wilbur
McFeely of The Conference Board underlined the importance of
that experience. And what topped off my excitement was a new
book by Warren Bennis (with Philip Slater), *The Temporary
Society*. The book confirmed something that I had begun to suspect,
something that has influenced me greatly in the twenty years
since—chiefly, that the traditional pyramid model of the organization must give way to more effective organic systems.

The experience I'd had was sitting on a task force that
actually produced something of value. Bill McFeely gave a speech in
which he predicted task force management to be the wave of the
future. And Warren Bennis wrote that the organization of the future
would consist of many temporary problem-solving groups that
would coexist with the permanent structure.

The task force I sat on was the first such participation I'd ever
experienced. I'd been on committees, of course, but most committees are exploratory and advisory bodies—quite different from a task
force, which often cuts across lines of authority. Some background
is helpful. In the early 1960s, the Research Institute of America
designed a program, to be sold by its salespeople, that would help
small- to medium-size companies train and develop their managers.
The managers who were enrolled in the program could take it on
their own, or trainers could use it as the basis for a continuing
course. The backbone of the program was a weekly newsletter called
Report To Members (RTM). *RTM* was supposed to offer current

advice and techniques to managers. It was to be both topical and timely.

The actual *RTM* was a hodgepodge. No one quite knew what to do with it. It became a collection of sometimes disparate articles that were printed because the editor had nothing else available. And it didn't help that some of the editors who assumed responsibility for the newsletter at one time or another knew nothing about managing.

By the summer of 1967, institute management decided to take action since renewals, understandably, were rotten. But top management wasn't sure what to do about *RTM*, so they assembled a task force—and no one was even sure exactly how to do that. (Task forces were seldom used in those days, and there wasn't much in the way of guidance on how to use them.) Even so, calling a group of people together and saying, "Fix it," proved to be quite sensible. At first glance, the people who were called together may not have seemed quite appropriate, but, in a task force, the membership is often interdisciplinary, so it was fine. There was a lawyer, an economist, a management expert, a business tax specialist, a sales trainer, and two or three general writers.

As a group, we made some interesting administrative decisions. As often happens in a task force, we represented more than one department. It seemed onerous to try to juggle our relationships with the two department heads involved, so we told their boss that we'd prefer to report directly to him—as it turned out, a smart, instinctive decision. The second significant decision involved our own leadership. A move to have a permanent chair—a resort to the familiar—was set aside in favor of a rotating chair. The reason for doing this was inspired. While the task force was in charge of *RTM*, all members of the group would have to contribute to it on a weekly basis to keep it going. The best way to ensure that everyone would indeed keep up a regular contribution was to require each person to serve two weeks as editor and chair of the task force. If each member knew that, as editor, he or she would have to depend on the others, then that person was sure to submit a weekly article while the others were running the newsletter. You can hardly depend on the others to do their jobs if they can't depend on you.

Our first major decision was to determine the kind of publication *RTM* should be. It had been nothing to anyone. Now it had to be everything to everyone. And that was going to be difficult since our readership was made up of high-level executives, plant managers, controllers, engineers, sales managers, and marketing managers, to cite just a few. What was the one thing they had in common? Behavior, effective behavior—theirs and that of their subordinates. So, how about a publication that would be devoted to telling them how to be more effective in dealing with others and how to assist their employees in working more effectively? At that time, to my knowledge, there was no such publication going to managers. There were professionals writing for other professionals but not to practitioners in lay language.

In five months, the task force produced an entirely new publication—and a new department. The group recommended to management that a new department be formed to publish the new report and that I be its editor. The design for *RTM,* incidentally, would be adopted later for another publication, *Personal Report for the Executive,* one of the most popular and profitable products RIA ever produced.

RTM was an admirably successful venture, especially considering that we did all the right things without knowing we were doing them. We *sensed* we were right. We insisted on a high degree of autonomy, made possible by reporting to an executive high enough to give us an umbrella of authority. We were interdisciplinary and interfunctional, and those characteristics contributed to a decision that was not parochial. We chose our own leadership—not necessary for a task force to be legitimate, but helpful. We saw ourselves as temporary, and we selected our own termination date. And we believed we had the responsibility to develop an operating mechanism—the new department and staff—that would ensure the implementation of our decision.

In my working experience, I had known only the highly stratified, rigidly functional, pyramidal type of operation, which still prevails. This was my first taste of workplace democracy, and I was intoxicated. A few weeks later, I picked up a newsletter that quoted Wilbur McFeely of The Conference Board, the prestigious business organization, as saying that task force management was the wave of the future. I was having my religious experience confirmed.

About the same time (isn't it marvelous how great minds run parallel?), the Bennis book came out. (I say Bennis because, though Philip Slater contributed sections, it was Bennis's part of the book that proved more relevant to me.) Consider this key quote: "Democracy becomes a functional necessity whenever a social system is competing for survival under conditions of chronic change." In 1968, business executives were agreeing that, indeed, the only constant was change. Bennis gave us a voice from the wilderness.

He defined some of the characteristics of democracy: free flowing communication throughout (Likert's System 4), consensus decision making, "the idea that *influence* is based on technical competence and knowledge rather than on the vagaries of personal whims and prerogatives of power," and a "human bias," which permits emotional expression and recognizes the inevitability of conflict as well as the need to work out the conflict on rational grounds.

Bennis proposed an adaptive organization made up of rapidly changing temporary systems that permit an organization to bring to bear the most effective resources for solving problems. "These will be," according to Bennis, "task forces composed of groups of relative strangers with diverse professional backgrounds and skills organized around problems to be solved. The groups will be arranged on an organic rather than mechanical model, meaning that they will evolve in response to a problem rather than to preset, programmed expectations. People will be evaluated not vertically according to rank and status, but flexibly according to competence. Organizational charts will consist of project groups rather than stratified functional groups."

In a meager way, I've tried to portray my excitement over what seemed to be a convergence of experience, philosophy, and technique. I was not alone in envisioning a radical revolution in the way organizations were structured and how they were managed. At the time I describe, we were in what I call the group era—massive experimentation with people in small groups: sensitivity training, encounter groups, T-groups, and the like. The research of the 1950s and 1960s was being validated by much of this group activity. Consensus decision making was touted as superior to the products of individual thinking or majority vote. We were beginning to understand clearly the dynamics of small groups, and the task force was generally considered to be a small group that made consensus decisions.

Concurrently, there was much published on systems. By the early 1970s, *systems* had become a buzzword. It was widely agreed that most people in this country worked in systems that were, to one degree or another, closed—that is, not healthily and broadly interacting with their environment. In a closed system, both wisdom and decisions come down from the top. But the new breed of systems thinkers described a better, more responsive system: the open system. Its boundaries with the environment were permeable and flexible, although firm enough to retain an identity. An open system responded to stimuli throughout, not just at the top, and it was far more effectively geared to deal with fast change than was the closed system.

Perhaps you can understand how some of us thought we were poised on the threshold of a new era, one in which organizations would be more adaptive, more responsive, and more flexible. It was obviously, as McFeely and Bennis suggested, the age of the temporary system.

Fired by the implications of all that I saw and heard, I wrote my first book, *Your Role in Task Force Management*, published in 1972. Despite its rather focalized title, I was sure that, given the temper of the time, it would be a best-seller. I envisioned organizations in which the competition would be so keen for seats on interesting task forces that a reward for good service on one such group would be coveted membership in an even more important group. Merit increases and other rewards for good performance would be decided by one's permanent manager and by the task force head. Individual performance evaluations would be the responsibility not only of a person's boss but also of group peers. I even suggested that the task force leader be appraised by the group members, who would determine whether they would serve with him or her again.

On the crest of the wave of the future, I quoted British author Anthony Burgess, who wrote in an article for *The New York Times*, "I home to America as to a country more stimulating than depressing. The future of mankind is being worked out there." And I borrowed a quote from the provocative book that Jean-François Revel of France authored, *Without Marx or Jesus:* "The revolution of the twentieth century will take place in the United States. It is only there that it can happen. And it has already begun." After praising the almost universal usefulness of the task force, I agreed with both, and wrote: "The future is already here. It is up to us to make it work."

Now you can take a deep breath. I was working up to some kind of climax, wasn't I? My book went to the shredder in 1984 after having achieved a sale of about 1,500 copies. The Japanese started the revolution without us, after having gotten so turned on by all the work Americans did on participative management and consensus decision making. The Europeans, especially the Scandinavians, began to increase output with self-directed work teams, which have been pioneered in the United States. The American automative industry looked at the Volvo phenomenon with some interest, and the United Auto Workers sent a delegation to check it out. Their finding: It wasn't compatible with our work culture. A dog food plant opened in Kansas with democratic work teams and apparently was such a success that the experiment had to be terminated. It was just too threatening to the management in the corporation's other divisions.

Warren Bennis, in his book, had expressed a fear that I chose to discount: American managers would not have much tolerance for the ambiguity created in an organization that mixes permanent and temporary structures. People want a clear line of authority, a fixed office, and a nameplate with title on the door. When you're moving around from group to group, from boss to boss, and from responsibility to responsibility, with no secure place on the chart, you may feel anxious and insecure. And one other manifestation of ambiguity wasn't taken seriously: What was the role of a manager when the employee group managed itself? The reduction in or disappearance of managerial prerogatives simply scared the hell out of a lot of people.

Twenty years after I saw a revolution in progress, do I still believe it will happen? Yes, for the following reasons.

Competition. I'm told that it takes an average of twice as long for Americans to bring a product to market as it does for some of our global competitors. Whatever the added time, it's unnecessarily long because we are, by and large, wedded to sequential decision making. Everyone has a say, but usually in sequence—research and development to engineering to production to finance to marketing and back again at each step when someone has a reservation. Simultaneous decision making by product task forces and project teams would hasten the process.

Lack of Opportunity. I think it was back in the early 1970s when Peter Drucker began to warn us that the baby boom had produced more potentially ambitious people than we had roles for in our organizations. There just wasn't much room at the top in our pyramids for all the people who wanted to be there. A flattened organization with plenty of opportunities in task forces and project teams was supposed to substitute for real authority and responsibility—or what used to pass for it in the middle layers. And I suspect that all this talk about entrepreneurship in organizations is an indication of the need for that flattening out.

Work Culture. Rensis Likert made a case almost thirty years ago that people tend to be more productive in environments and organizations in which they have a say in issues that affect them. Today I write confidently, although more cautiously than before, that we are steadily evolving toward a more democratic or, at least, a more participative work culture. Even General Motors acknowledges the evolution with its Saturn project in Tennessee with its workplace democracy and self-directed work teams.

So when I am asked whether the temporary society will indeed be permanent, my aha! has been tempered to a long ahhhhhhh, followed by a short but rather unemphatic yes. It is coming. But Bennis was right in his caution. And Bill McFeely's prediction, while not fulfilled in the 1970s or 1980s, has a better chance in the 1990s. It's awfully difficult to overcome the centuries-old confidence in the military-church model of organization and to overcome the bias toward the power that accrues to those toward the top.

Chapter 22

Why Management Development Doesn't Develop

*I*t's an awful reality: American business will invest billions of dollars this year to develop its supervisors and managers in what are presumably the most advanced management education programs in the world, and much of that money will simply go to waste—punching holes in water, as my Italian friends are fond of saying. The truth is painful, so the people who pay all that money for management training and development—management—don't care to talk about it, and the people who deliver it—trainers—are understandably reluctant to acknowledge it.

Most people who work in organizations today don't need me to tell them that bad management abounds. Managers are abrasive and insensitive toward subordinates, they fail to communicate, they punish instead of inspire, they present models of incompetence, they are arbitrary in their decisions, and they refuse to delegate, to cite just a few flaws. And many of those managers have attended courses and programs that tell them they shouldn't behave in any of those ways.

Every trainer and management consultant hears employees' war stories about their bosses. I've been hearing them for the twenty-eight years I've been in management development. If you give credence to even a small fraction of their complaints, you inevitably decide that many managers just don't seem to work right. In fact, you hear a lot of what historian Barbara Tuchman, in *The March of Folly,* calls *woodenheadedness*—self-defeating behavior at all levels of management.

Yet, for the years I've been in the field, management development has been big business in this country. Our training delivery

140

systems have become increasingly sophisticated. We have state-of-the-art classrooms, we use multimedia presentations, we've incorporated interactive video, we've streamlined and updated our curricula. Nevertheless, many trainers share my experience; managers are still asking us the same basic questions they asked us ten years ago: "Where's the progress?"

Rather, where's the problem? When training fails, the blame is usually—sometimes appropriately—laid at the door of the training department. It is true that many people delivering management development have never managed a day in their lives. For them it's a classroom exercise, which may or may not reflect the problems or deal with the concerns of people on the work scene. Many trainers have come from the public sector and know little of the realities of running a business. They are input oriented: Their priority is the design of a program. They may have little interest in measuring the output—what happens as a result of the training—and even if they do have that interest, they probably don't have measurement tools.

I never have been known to be reluctant to take my colleagues to the woodshed, but I also insist on pointing the finger at management, which shares the responsibility for the poor results of management training. Management's commitment to development is often poor, for at least three reasons: Management doesn't understand the development process, doesn't believe it works, and, in some cases, doesn't want it to work.

When an executive describes management development as soft stuff, I know that he or she doesn't understand it. The meaning of that familiar phrase is that learning about management methods and leadership skills is similar to nailing gelatin to the wall. Computing or quantitative decision making is hard stuff. There are definite rules and techniques. But supervising people, well, that's spongy and difficult to categorize.

The fact is that we in the management field have very clear ideas about the kinds of management and leadership to which employees respond favorably, and by favorably I mean productively. We understand the behavior of people at work, and we can therefore advise managers on techniques that will enhance their subordinates' motivating forces. We can train managers to communicate more effectively with employees, even to correct and to criticize employees' behavior so that motivation increases rather than decreases. We can offer recommendations to managers that will help them intensify the commitment of their people through employees' ownership of goals. Everything we have to offer has been validated by research and experience through several decades. And some of us who have managed can testify to our own success in using these approaches.

Management is not soft stuff. On the contrary, we know what we need to know to achieve greater productivity from employees and consequent better showings on bottom lines. We have the concepts and the techniques, and we know how to practice them.

Another reason for management's weak commitment to management development is that they do not really believe it works. Periodically, someone will tell me that he followed a recommendation I made in one of my books and that it actually worked. Not long ago, in a training program, I assigned the managers an action plan that involved their praising an employee who was doing something well. When they came together the following week and reported, some of the trainees were wide-eyed in astonishment. The employees had responded positively, and some even had thanked the managers for noticing.

There is a great deal of skepticism about the efficacy of a management training program, and some of it is justified. Much of the training is delivered under conditions that don't seem to relate to the real-world workplace. And it isn't uncommon to hear trainees say, "Well, this might work under ideal circumstances, but . . ." The content presented in the classroom has to relate to the working environment. If it doesn't (and many presenters don't know enough or are too inexperienced to make it happen), the necessary connection isn't established, so trainees may feel they have wasted their time. Both trainers and managements have flirted with fads and simplistic formulas; of course, they don't work well over the long run, so certain cynicism has built up. Nevertheless, it isn't hard to understand why people continue to look for the easy ways to do hard things, or why people espouse principles of good managing— universals—without really understanding that those principles are practiced one-to-one.

Another contributor to disbelief is the artificiality we create in our management training programs. In the more elaborate programs, there is a curriculum, just as in high school or college—thirteen courses and a certificate. Or we present what I call skills packages: two days of delegating, one day of communicating, four days of leadership, and so on. There is no system and no integration. They're basically "shoulds" that would be nice to do.

Over easy may be a good way to serve eggs, but it is a remarkably poor way to dish up management development. Most management skills are presented in bits and pieces, as discrete functions that may or may not be related.

In the face of such low expectations, why have management training? "Well," the answer is, "something just might rub off." Considering the annual bill for such training, it seems to be expensive serendipity.

Perhaps the most provocative statement I've made is that some managements don't want their training to be effective because what is traditionally taught in management development programs may contradict the corporate culture. In such cases, lip service is paid throughout the organization to the training, but, in fact, when the trainee returns to the work scene, he or she receives the unmistakable message, "Forget what you've been taught. That's not the way we do things here." This is the ultimate travesty: that which is taught not only doesn't relate but is considered subversive.

If training is subversive, it shouldn't be offered. The explanation in this instance is that it is offered for competitive reasons. People want it; people expect it; others are doing it. Small wonder there is so much cynicism in this field.

Management development can be effective, and certainly in some cases it is effective. Enlightened managements and training professionals have combined their resources in some organizations to make their investments of time and money pay off. But they have found that, if they are not to establish a charm school for managers, they must act in accordance with hard realities. For example, development is not selective; it must be pervasive. You start at the top and go through each level of the hierarchy. Unfortunately, many top managements think that management skills are no longer relevant to them. One training director sarcastically described his executive group this way: "At this level, they know everything and need nothing." In fact, many executive development programs have little or nothing in them about managing, as if the executive trainees actually believed they don't need their skills sharpened. In one workshop I conducted, the CEO sat on the side, observing, but refusing to participate. I asked my contact person why the top level had not been included. His answer: "It would threaten them."

When top management orders the program and monitors it without participating, they suggest that the trainees are dummies.

The second hard reality is that training must be conducted within a system—in a context. As I continue to insist, management is not a series of disconnected acts. Everything a manager does has some impact, positive or negative, on employees' motivation and commitment. Motivation therefore provides a context for training managers in leadership skills and management methods. Simply throwing skillls packages at managers out of context virtually guarantees that, within a couple of weeks, most of what was taught in the classroom will be forgotten.

An ancillary point is that adults must be given a reason for learning. You can't treat them like children who are force-fed knowledge. Yet we often do. Managing motivation is a good reason, if what the trainees learn will make their jobs easier and more effective.

The third hard reality is that training and development must be ongoing. Management must give trainees the opportunity to apply in the workplace what they have learned in the development program. Managers must be equipped to coach the management trainees on the job and to show them how the concepts and techniques must be applied. In time, everyone in management becomes not only a trainee but a trainer of others. In effect, the walls of the classroom disappear. It is simply an extension of the workplace.

The last reality is that the reward system must encourage and reinforce the application of the new knowledge and skills. Managers from top to bottom must be partners with training professionals in designing the kind of training that will indeed result in the managerial effectiveness desired. There must be an alignment of the reward system to reinforce the learning; the retention curve is everyone's enemy. Adults need feedback when they try to apply what they've brought back from the training room and they need rewards when they have been successful. When people feel rewarded for what they do, they'll repeat the behavior.

When everyone in the organization is learning essentially the same values and skills, when the message throughout is that the trainees will be rewarded for applying the skills they have learned, and when what goes on in the classroom deals realistically with the problems and concerns that managers have on the work scene, some amazing results will occur. The organization will see a surge in the effectiveness of its people. And everyone will be traveling in the same direction. Otherwise, management development will continue to be a self-fulfilling prophecy. We will design and administer it in such a way that it cannot possibly work, and then we will proclaim it to be of doubtful value—of doubtful and expensive value.

Of course, I suppose there's always the possibility that something will rub off.

Chapter 23

Building Power Without Corruption

I know what Lord Acton said about power: "Power corrupts, and absolute power corrupts absolutely." Considering that you can't get anything done without having power if you're in an organization, I've begun to think that his comment sounds nice but has little practical value. Of course you must also remember that Lord Acton lived during a time when, to get attention, you uttered aphorisms. As the gun people say, guns don't kill people; people kill people. Nice distinction. I suppose the same holds true for power: Power doesn't corrupt; people corrupt people. Another nice distinction.

Well, it's an abstruse point, and I'm generally into abstruse points only when I've had a few drinks. But it's only eight in the morning, and that's early, even for me. So I'm going to have to hold to a more realistic position: If you want to get anything done, you need to have power and influence. That's the reality. And people who disdain power, I'm convinced, are people who don't have it and probably don't know how to get it. A lot of people who have power pretend they don't. And power is seldom a module in management training. It's almost as if it were simply not respectable to acknowledge that power not only exists but that is is necessary.

When I was in organizational life, I never knew much about power, except that I didn't have much of it. Like many other people, I relied on my competence. I'd like to think that there is justice in the world and that you can't get far without competence. But seeing too many cases of the Peter Principle has cured me of that. It has become clear to me that competence by itself is usually not enough to win you what you want.

146

But like anyone else coming out of corporate life, I knew a lot about power. I have climbed into the ring a few times, and I found out what it is to go down for the count. So when an editor asked me to do a book about power, I could show some scars to prove that I had some familiarity with the subject.

In researching the book, I began to look at all the kinds of power I had seen demonstrated in thirty years. I identified twelve sources or kinds of power that are available to almost anyone who wants to take the time and trouble to build a legitimate power base. In fact, I was amazed to see how readily available much power is. I'll start with the kind of power that I think is essential for a durable power base.

Competence. We've all seen people who did not seem to have the competence to be where they are. But I would venture that most if not all of them started out being good at something. They just go further than their competence. For most people, their first hint of power is being considered good at knowing what they are about. However, if you want to be noticed, you have to promote yourself as well as being competent. Some people promote themselves even though they don't have much competence. I spent thirty years being pretty good at what I was doing, and I recall getting maybe two job offers the whole time. That wasn't the case with some others I knew who were mostly show and little go. They seemed to have headhunters camping on their doorsteps.

Personal. These people don't stand alone at a meeting or a reception; people seen drawn to them. They are magnetic. It's in the way they stand, the way they walk, the way they talk, and yes, even in the way they dress. They project not only competence but confidence in themselves. By contrast, I've been the invited speaker at functions, showed up during the reception, and had no one notice me. I remember one public figure who had immense personal power: Jack Kennedy. I was in a church one Sunday morning in Maine when he walked in. He filled that church with his presence.

Assigned-Delegated. If you don't have enough power in your own situation, you look for it. One place to look is your boss and the things he or she doesn't like to do or doesn't do well. Eugene Jennings wrote a book twenty years ago, *The Mobile Manager,* that is still valid. Its message was to become a crucial subordinate to your boss. Look for task forces to be a part of. They're underused, but they are power vehicles because, as a participant, you often enjoy much more authority than you would as an individual. Of course, the problem is being able to distinguish between simply doing someone's dirty work and shining as a hero when you've done something that no one else wanted to do—or could do. Many people have the it's-not-my-job perspective, but people in a power track sniff out work that isn't properly theirs—work that will give them a chance to achieve and to be visible.

Associative. You may have been associating with the turkeys, but if you want power, join the eagles. If you fly with them often enough, people will assume you are one. Identify the power centers in your organization. Get acquainted with them. Seek their counsel on your career or on organizational issues. If you're in the conference room when bigwig walks in, you'll notice that others hang back. You shouldn't. Stride confidently across the room and start a conversation with bigwig. Look for a mentor or sponsor among the power people. If you are associated with a powerful person, you'll find some of it rubbing off on you. The danger: If you become too closely associated with a power center who loses power, you may suffer also. It's good to have other sources of power.

Resources. Find out what others need and can't get easily, then supply it. A friend of mine worked for a company that wanted to initiate self-development brochures for supervisors. He had been a supervisor for several years, so his stock went way up. Remember how, back in the early days of computers, the EDP (electronic data processing) people were priests in the temple? It takes some sniffing about sometimes to find a niche for yourself and perhaps some training and education. But if you're the guru on the mountaintop to whom people have to make pilgrimages, you have a lot of power. Another friend of mine educated herself in desktop publishing at a time when it was an esoteric subject. She knew that eventually there would be an interest in her office in that function. There was, and she shined.

Alliance. There is strength in numbers, as long as those numbers don't appear subversive. One group of managers in a training class of mine discovered this happily. They were seven branch managers who complained that their boss in the home office didn't give them the attention, support, and respect they felt they deserved when they talked with him. Each field manager had been conducting business with the home office individually. But after spending several months together in a management development program, they began to suspect that the togetherness in the classroom could be extended to the work scene. From that point on, they conferred among themselves on common issues and approached the boss as a group—or sent a representative. They were astonished at the newfound respect they enjoyed. There's sometimes a temptation, when you have a good idea, to go it alone because you want the idea identified with you. But it may serve your proposal better to line up your allies in advance and to look for people to do favors for. Those IOUs will come in handy someday.

Reward. Most managers readily acknowledge that they have reward power over subordinates. They can give raises, privileges, and perks. But expand your thinking. Anytime you can help somebody to look good, make recommendations about others, or endorse their ideas, you may be seen as providing rewards. And that's especially true when you have great credibility—when you enjoy respect from those who will listen to your recommendations. Don't forget those opportunities to praise and compliment others, even though you are not required or expected to. Gratuitous praise is a special reward. Once again, you'll collect some IOUs that may be helpful to you later.

Professional. You build your power base within the organization by your activities outside it. If you belong to a professional association and are active in it, the esteem you enjoy from fellow professionals may convince your co-workers that you are to be taken seriously. Even if you're not a professional, you can look for voluntary, charitable, or civic groups in which you'll be associating with influential people. Again, their respect for you may have impact on the people you work with and for. Look for opportunities to publish articles, perhaps even a book, or to give speeches. Then make sure that your house publication plays up your outside activities. One caveat: Some organizations frown on their key people indulging in outside activities. It's a very myopic view, but if it exists, this kind of power won't help you much—except perhaps to get noticed by a more progressive company.

Availability. Somewhat akin to resources power is availability. It's being in the right place at the right time with the right mix of skills. You may not be the only or even the primary source, as you might be as a resource, but you are there. I've known perfectly decent but not extraordinary people who received big career boosts simply because they made it convenient for theirs bosses to pick them for a job. In some cases, they anticipated their bosses' needs; in others they were just lucky. But in the words of one rock star, "I've worked all my life to become an overnight success."

Autocratic. Entrepreneurs sometimes have it. Rescuers and raiders sometimes get it. Look for opportunities when people are floundering or demoralized or terribly frustrated, and they might welcome a rescuer who assumes control. For the most part, however, you won't be able to acquire autocratic power. In today's culture it is getting harder and harder to build. But if you work for an organization headed by an autocratic executive, the closer you get to him or her the more of that power may rub off. When you can boast, as an acquaintance of mine does, that you have instant access to the great man, you can't help feeling that you have some power, although it will always flow from his generosity. An autocrat can give it; an autocrat can shut it off.

Charismatic-Visionary. I don't know how one develops charismatic power, although I have seen it firsthand. When I was a young fellow in military school, there would occasionally emerge a seventeen-year-old who would be able naturally to make unruly adolescents do what he wanted them to do. And later, I worked for a charismatic boss. It was exhilarating and frustrating. He was an exciting leader but without great skill as a manager.

Everyone can work on visionary power, and everyone can have a vision of what the organization or department can and should do. And people will, as they say, buy into it and want to work with you to achieve it if you have the power of charisma.

Position. Soon after a promotion, you can become disillusioned to find that positions often offer little power in themselves. Even Harry Truman found that the office of president carries much prestige but deceptively little power. But you can build the power of your position by expanding your influence. People on the power track are empire builders. They pick up an increment of responsibility here and there, and, after a time, they've expanded their power enormously—a little at a time.

By now you've discovered that, while there are twelve sources or kinds of power available in some degree to most people, the twelve are not entirely separate and distinct. They are interrelated. For example, to build position power you could utilize a number of other sources. And if you want to be personally powerful, your self-confidence may flow from your having successfully drawn on, say, assigned-delegated power and from your having achieved creditable things.

In my experience, people who build enduring power bases use more than one block. And they maintain their power bases. On the power track, there's no taking anything for granted. But the important message is that almost anyone in an organization can build some power and, indeed, must if he or she is going to get anything done.

I will, however, give Lord Acton partial points. I agree that absolute power does corrupt, but I don't know anyone these days who has it—no one in my circle, certainly. As for just plain power, it's time, I think, to stop denying, or at least camouflaging, its necessity. If you want to get anything done, you must have it. It may go against tradition to show people formally how to get organized, but to do so will increase their effectiveness.

Chapter 24

Let's Stop Emphasizing Morale

I wouldn't want anyone to misunderstand me: I'm totally in favor of happiness on the job. And making employees happy seems to be a stated goal of many managements. But in getting the work out, I'm just not sure how important the happiness of employees is. Although I'm in favor of everyone being happy, I am not a member of the human relations school of managing. Their tenet is that employers should be nice to employees because that will make them happy, and happy employees work better. Well, all we know about happy employees is that they are happy. Whether they do more work than employees who are not happy is not certain. Besides, the human relations approach was the rationale for paternalism, which is not necessarily being nice to people.

But, admittedly, in the minds of many managers, there is a definite correlation between the happiness of employees and how much work bosses can get out of them. In any management development program, you'll hear management trainees complaining about the negative effects of oppressive or incompetent leadership. You can't expect employees to perform well when their morale is low, and so on, and so on. For these rationalizing managers, the bad news is that we've never established an essential relationship between morale and motivation. No one that I know of has been able to prove in psychological research that people whose morale is low tend to produce less than people whose morale is high.

I once worked for a happy department. I don't believe there was one miserable person in the group. Why should there have been? We were pretty well paid. No one seemed to care when we came to work or went home or returned from lunch, or whether we came in at all. The boss practiced an extreme form of laissez-faire management, and he definitely believed in human relations. I remember some very nice chats we had when he made his rounds. He was indeed a charming man. But what I do not remember is whether there was much emphasis on quantity and quality of work. In fact, my lingering impression is that a lot of the work we did—we were writers—was eminently forgettable. It was just about the most relaxed and contented department you'll ever expect to find. But a person who believed in high standards and who wished for a stimulating atmosphere was bound to be disappointed with this department.

A few years later, I was confronted by a startling contrast. I was the head of a department that was due to be terminated at the end of two years, and everyone knew that we'd all be out of work at the end of that time. There was, as the French would say, a *sauve qui peut* attitude—save yourself if you can. That was sheer magnanimity on the part of the rest of us. As people transferred out, those of us who remained had to pick up their portion of the work because the work output was expected to stay constant.

Contributing to the declining morale was the widespread belief among employees that top management didn't know what it was doing, wouldn't know competence from incompetence, and didn't much care. That was an exaggeration, of course, but since top management seldom communicated with employees, we had no way of knowing anything else.

You might assume that morale was about as low as it could get. There was a lot of gallows humor; yet, we insisted on maintaining high standards of productivity and quality. We cut no corners and gave no quarter. From what I could determine, the output from our department was the highest in the company. You cannot maintain that kind of result without people's motivation being very high. There was no such thing as my trying to put on a happy face for them. I gave them all the news I had, even though most of it was unpleasant. I shared their criticism of management. My group was fully informed, fully aware. And they worked hard. I have never seen a group in similar adverse circumstances more committed.

It's a lovely paradox. People who enjoy high morale produce in a mediocre fashion, and those whose morale is virtually nonexistent maintain high levels of quantity and quality of output. My experience confounds conventional wisdom.

Although it's true that no definite correlation has been determined between morale and motivation, I suspect that a good case could be made that a prolonged depression in morale will hurt motivation, and, in turn, productivity. After a time, work simply requires more energy under conditions that are not pleasant. There's a leaden feeling as you wake up in the morning and say to yourself, "My God, I have to go back to that place today." One of the factors that made the situation in the second example more tolerable, I think, was the limited time period. We knew that in two years it would all be over—not that that was a happy thought. After all, we'd all be out of a job. But the suffering would be over. I've always said that if you put me in chains, I could somehow put up with it if you also told me there was a limit to how long I would be there.

Many people working in organizations these days are in chains. They put up with poor supervision, limited satisfaction with their work, insensitivity of management, and stupid decisions that affect them. Almost anyone in an organization is at the mercy of forces and people over which he or she has little influence. Faced with just such a frustration, I once wrote an article about how one's career is often limited by ineptitude of others. In my case, I was employed in production by a company in which the marketing staff was not, in my judgment, competent. Sales were declining, and they didn't know what to do about it. And they wouldn't seek any help. As a result, the revenues decreased and so did the chances of salary increases for the rest of us.

Ironically, happy groups often anesthetize themselves against unpleasant realities. In my group insurance days, about which I've written elsewhere in this book, I worked at one point with a company general agent who believed in maintaining a paternalistic, happy, family environment. During one sales meeting with his agents, I gave them the bad news that one of our products was not as competitive as it could be, and that there were certain conditions under which they could sell it successfully and other conditions under which they shouldn't waste their time. The general agent complained about me to the home office, and I was censured.

I had disturbed the tranquility. The truth may indeed set you free (and in this case would have given you a chance to make more money) but not necessarily if you work for a boss who insists that everyone be happy.

In another relationship, the general agent was equally paternalistic. He represented the cheerleading school of management. Every Saturday morning, he called his flock together and exhorted them in his sales sermons to excel. His gatherings were priceless opportunities to raise skills levels. Instead they became pep rallies. It reminds one of some of the companies that, every morning, used to hold rallies at which their salespeople sang fight songs. They even had a recessional during which the salespeople sang all the way out to the nearest coffee shop.

In a happy environment, the emphasis is on what social psychologist Frederick Herzberg terms *hygiene* or *maintenance* factors. They are *dissatisfiers,* which, in Herzberg's lexicon, means that they don't motivate or satisfy; but if they are not present, they will cause dissatisfaction. In short, people who have them will not necessarily be happy, but if they don't have them, they will probably be unhappy. Before Herzberg's two-factor theory became known, many people thought that some of the following factors did indeed enhance motivation:

- *Supervision:* The kindly, caring, fatherly supervisor.
- *Company policy and administration:* Don't you worry your little heads about such matters; leave them to us.
- *Positive working conditions:* Well lighted, clean, neat, attractive. Don't you love to come to work in a well-designed, colorful environment?
- *Salary:* We pay you, so you should be happy, content, and loyal.
- *Interpersonal relations:* It's a happy place; don't be a troublemaker.
- *Job security:* If you are nice and don't cause problems, you might stay here forever. (However, even in the most paternalistic companies, job security is becoming history.)

In philosophy, we used to distinguish between essence and accident. The essence is what makes something what it is and distinguishes it from everything else. The accident, or accidental, is the outward manifestation of the essence, like red hair or tallness. In a happy environment, the emphasis seems to be on the accidental. In contrast, Herzberg has made a good case for the essence—the motivation rooted in the work being done, in achievement, and in growth on the job.

Don't get me wrong. If I had all those motivators, I'd rather be happy than unhappy. I like morale on the high side. And I'd prefer not to have to pay a price for my happiness—a price such as pretending or conforming. But as to the significance of employees' happiness itself, well, happy employees are happy employees are happy employees. Gertrude Stein couldn't have said it better.

Chapter 25

Simple Is Hard,
Complex Is Easy,
Simplistic Is Impossible

"*O*ver here," Fritz Roethlisberger used to say, referring to the Harvard Business School where he taught, "we make complex things easy; over there," pointing to the main Harvard campus on the other side of the Charles River, "they make simple things complex." Roethlisberger, a member of Elton Mayo's team at Hawthorne and a pioneer in the field of organizational behavior, followed his own guidelines. His work is eminently readable and admirably straightforward. But maybe he pared down his prose too much. These days, who reads Fritz Roethlisberger? How many people know who he was?

In management today, we seem, for some mysterious reason, to tend toward the complex or the simplistic. Simple is mistrusted— suspect. Take my field of motivation. From my surveys, I've concluded that most management training in employee motivation and productivity uses either Maslow or Herzberg as its theory base. Most people are familiar with Maslow's hierarchy of needs. From the lowest need, which is physiological, a person moves up the hierarchy to satisfy safety needs, then on to those related to belongingness and love, and then to esteem, until finally he or she is working to fill a growth need, self-actualization. Maslow says that a person feels a particular need only when the needs lower in the hierarchy are predominantly satisfied. Thus, a person probably won't seek the esteem of others until he or she has satisfied the yearning for belongingness and love. I personally doubt that is true, and experimental projects to validate the hierarchy have been inconclusive. I've never been able to explain to managers how to recognize which need an employee might be working on at a given time. And I'm not at all sure what constitutes a need predominantly satisfied. Maslow is complicated.

Frederick Herzberg's two-factor theory also is complicated. There are ambiguities such as the role of salary. He says it is not a motivator; yet, if it is a recognition of achievement, it is. And there are gaps in his list of motivators. Overall, however, the two-factor theory, as far as it goes, has been validated through thirty years of application. Yet, as a basic explanation of human behavior, it is complex.

In my work in motivation, I use a startlingly simple theory: Expectancy Theory. Some psychology students may know it as social learning theory. It states that human behavior is a function of (1) the value of the reward the doer perceives as coming from the chosen behavior and (2) the doer's expectation that the reward is attainable without undue risk or effort. You do things because they are valuable to you. And you do them because you have confidence that you can be successful in doing them. The theory applies to your choice of a career, a job, a task, or what you'll have for lunch. When you make a choice, you choose the option that provides you with the most valuable reward, whether that is money, or satisfaction, or achievement, or just plain physical gratification. However, you have to be convinced that the reward is attainable through reasonable effort. Most people will not take immoderate risks or work superhumanly to get what they want.

Expectancy Theory is so simple and practical. Kurt Lewin, the famous psychologist, used to say, "There is nothing so practical as a good theory." For purposes of management, Expectancy Theory is marvelously simple and practical. Managers are in a position to increase the value of the work for employees, and they can help increase the employees' expectations of getting what they value from the work. On that foundation, you can build a whole management system, all designed to make the work more rewarding and doable.

Simple is not easy. Simple is hard. Managing is hard. As I've often said, management principles are few and relatively simple to grasp. They are universal, but the practice of management is one-to-one. I can convince you of the desirability of delegating, but don't delegate the same way and the same tasks to everyone.

Years ago, my staff and I at the Research Institute of America demonstrated just how hard simple can be. Our newsletter for managers, *Personal Report for the Executive,* was known for its straightforward, uncomplicated style. It looked almost effortless— so much so that freelance writers continually asked to submit articles to us. They were deceived into thinking that, in our type of writing, all one had to do was to place the sheet of paper into the typewriter and an article would practically write itself. In fact, seldom did a freelance writer satisfy our specifications and standards.

The *Personal Report* style had been forged over much time. All the copy submitted by staffers was well worked over in editorial meetings, where the standards gradually evolved. The person who rewrote and edited the original copy knew those standards. Eventually, the copy in print all sounded pretty much alike, except for some idiosyncrasies of the writers. Just as in the touch of a telegrapher, every writer leaves his or her signature. After a time, and after much hard work, the writing looked effortless. We had achieved what the Roman poet Horace referred to as "artful artlessness."

Anyone who teaches writing can tell you that the first attempts by trainees result in complicated prose. It's unorganized. It may ramble. It often seems to have no cohesion and no discernible sequence. A lot of published writing is that way. A prime example is the average professional periodical; many contributions are nearly unreadable. It's easier to be complicated. Some of the most difficult writing I have to do is a descriptive or autobiographical paragraph of 100 words or less. I labor over that. As the famous orator (whose name is lost to me) said, after having been invited to prepare a speech, "Do you want a long speech or a short one? A long speech I can have ready in three days, a short one will probably take a week."

As I have pointed out in talking about motivation, training has become a very complicated affair; the basics are not popular. In the work I've done in the field of motivation—work based on Expectancy Theory—there's not a lot of interest because it's simple motivation from A to Z. But my lack of success in promoting the simple sparked one comment from a friend who, I think, is more realistic than cynical: "Call it something like Superpracticon Managerial Success Analyzer, invent a grid (everyone likes to plot something on a grid), develop an interactive videodisc, print lots of handouts, charge several thousand dollars for it, and you'll do better." Probably.

I lament the passing of the simplicity of Transactional Analysis. As Eric Berne described it, it is a wonderfully basic explanation of human interaction. You'll recall that there are three behavior modes: Child, Parent, and Adult, and most people slip in and out of all three. There are complementary transactions, such as child-parent, and there are crossed transactions, such as parent-adult. Complementary transactions achieve their purpose and make the participants feel OK; Crossed transactions get in the way of understanding and cooperation, and probably one of the communicators feels discounted, not OK. TA doesn't provide a universal explanation for every aspect of human behavior, but it provides some realistic bases. In a very short time using the TA model, you could train employees—especially those who meet the public, such as passenger agents and retail sales personnel—to deal with the various kinds of behavior they encounter.

Obviously, TA was too simple. First thing you know, it was being combined with Gestalt therapy, and the behavioral variations proliferated. It became a very complicated affair, one that could no longer be taught in a day or two. To master this new "science" required a couple of years of study. I'm convinced that TA disappeared not because people saw it as another fad, but because it collapsed of its own weight.

Simple does not seem to be natural to us. We must invest it with complexity to make it credible.

One of the most effective training programs I ever encountered was astonishingly simple in its design. Although I experienced it thirty years ago, it could well be a model for today. The man responsible for it was Tom Watson, sales manager for the group insurance department of the Lincoln National Life Insurance Company. After World War II, the Lincoln decided to get into the group insurance business. Unfortunately, many of its large competitors had been in that business for a decade or two. They had their group insurance offices already placed in key cities around the country to help insurance agents and brokers place group policies. In some cities, the volume of business justified offices with multiple staff.

Tom's problem was that he had to get national coverage for the Lincoln in a few years, but he didn't have the means or the money to turn out group specialists en masse. And for the foreseeable future, the Lincoln's regional offices would, for the most part, consist of one man. Tom's one man would have to be able to work alone to achieve greater per capita production than his competitors' field people.

When you were hired, either by Tom or by one of the two division managers, you were told that your training would take place in the home office, and that you played a large role in determining how long training would take. Your incentive, of course, was to get out into the field as soon as you could to make a higher base salary and to enjoy commissions on all the business produced by your office.

In addition to being a trainee, you were an active working member of the home office staff. You started out learning to prepare group insurance proposals for the men in the field. Then you would be permitted to handle correspondence with the field offices and policyholders. There were several other departments you had to learn about, such as underwriting, policy issuance, renewal, and service. Once you had mastered proposals, it was up to you, as a trainee, to schedule your training sessions with the other department heads. You often had to negotiate the time. No one told you what to do or when to do it. You were constantly thinking about shortening your time in the home office.

You had extensive access to the sales manager, Tom. In fact, you were supposed to take advantage of every opportunity to sit in his office during his office conferences, even with the chairman of the board. The rule was, when you saw someone enter Tom's office, you were to join them. If Tom felt the conversation was not appropriate for you or not helpful, he would shake his head when you appeared at the door, and you'd go back to what you were doing.

For most people, the invitation was a tough one to take

advantage of. In those days, the levels of command were much more formalized and stratified than they are now. At first you didn't feel comfortable following Tom's visitors, especially the high-level ones, into his office. But when you failed to do so a few times, Tom let you know that sitting in on his conversations was part of the job. He didn't give you a second warning. If you failed to take initiative, to assert yourself, Tom decided that you would not work well on your own in the field. You were washed out of the training.

Finally, when every department head agreed that you were ready, you were on your way to the field—to some real money.

You can understand why Tom Watson fielded one of the best sales forces I ever have encountered. The training was real time and real life. You, the trainee, were in charge of it. You understood the reason for each segment of it. And during the training period, while you absorbed the values and the culture of the operation, you were frequently tested on your suitability to represent the Lincoln, not by exams, but by demonstrated skill in doing the work.

Today, we talk about how managers must take responsibility for the training of their people, how the best training resembles the work scene, how adults must have reasons for learning and opportunities to apply that learning. Tom's design met these needs long before corporate training became so "sophisticated."

If the simple is a challenge to us, the simplistic—reduction of a problem to a false simplicity by ignoring complicating factors— always has an appeal. Many people have considered the One Minute Manager series to be a good example of the simplistic. It has proved true in my case. A few years ago, after the second One Minute book by Ken Blanchard, and after the second film, I was invited by the Chamber of Commerce in an upstate New York city to conduct question-and-answer sessions during a one-day One Minute Manager festival. They planned to show one film in the morning and the other in the afternoon. I would be on after each film. And I was indeed on—for two hours after each. Most of those people asking questions had read the books and now had seen the films, and some had even done some training on the One Minute system. For a total of four hours, I did nothing but answer questions from the audience—questions relating to what they'd seen heard or what they had experienced back on the job. I've never forgotten that it took four hours for me to handle questions arising from the One Minute Manager.

The logic is puzzling. If you want someone to do something very quickly, the result will probably be complicated. It's much easier to produce complexity under time pressure. If you have longer, you can hope for simplicity. And if you don't mind risking getting nothing usable, settle for the simplistic.

Afterword

Heraclitus, the Greek philosopher, has remained famous for holding that the only constant is change. He taught his disciples that you cannot put your foot into the same river twice since the flow of water changes the river on a continuing basis. But there is ambiguity involved in this reality: The molecules of water may be different, but the composition of the substance remains the same. Thus, you place your foot into the same substance each time but into different molecules of that same substance.

With the Americans' love of the straightforward, the black and white, the either-or, many managers have adopted the Heraclitean perspective: The only constant is change. But the French, much more comfortable with ambiguity, caution us that the more things change the more they remain the same. Or in classic philosophical terms, we must be careful not to confuse essence and accident. Often, it is the outward appearance that changes, not the substance. Many people mistake the two, often to their regret.

It helps, therefore, to allow yourself to develop an appreciation of ambiguity, to distrust, or at least to question, what others so glibly accept, especially when it is termed *conventional wisdom*. You'll find yourself making better evaluations of situations and wiser decisions if you suggest that what others adopt without examination may be neither conventional nor wise. And life becomes much more interesting when, at times, you experience the wonder that Alice did when she climbed through the looking glass and saw everything in a different perspective.

Bibliography

Bennis, W., and Slater, P. *The Temporary Society*. New York: Harper & Row, 1968.

Berne, E. *Games People Play*. New York: Grove, 1964.

Blake, R., and Mouton, J. *The Managerial Grid III: The Key to Leadership Excellence*. (3rd ed.) Houston: Gulf Publishing, 1984.

Blanchard, K., and Johnson, S. *The One Minute Manager*. New York: Morrow, 1982.

Carlzon, J. *Moments of Truth*. Cambridge, Mass.: Ballinger, 1987.

Herzberg, F. *Work and the Nature of Man*. Cleveland: World, 1966.

Jennings, E. *The Mobile Manager*. Ann Arbor: University of Michigan Press, 1967.

Korda, M. *Power: How to Get It, How to Use It*. New York: Random House, 1975.

Kundera, M. *The Unbearable Lightness of Being*. New York: Harper & Row, 1984.

Lee, A. *Multivalent Man*. New York: Braziller, 1966.

Likert, R. *New Patterns of Management*. New York: McGraw-Hill, 1961.

Maccoby, M. *The Gamesman, The New Corporate Leaders*. New York: Simon & Schuster, 1977.

McGregor, D. *The Human Side of Enterprise*. New York: McGraw-Hill, 1960.

Marrow, A. *The Practical Theorist: The Life and Work of Kurt Lewin*. New York: Basic, 1969.

Maslow, A. *Motivation and Personality*. New York: Harper & Row, 1954.

Ouchi, W. *Theory Z: How American Business Can Meet the Japanese Challenge*. New York: Avon, 1982.

Peters, J., and Waterman, R. *In Search of Excellence.* New York: Harper & Row, 1982.

Quick, T. *Your Role in Task Force Management: The Dynamics of Corporate Change.* New York: Doubleday, 1972.

Quick, T. *The Persuasive Manager: How to Sell Yourself and Your Ideas.* Radnor, Penn.: Chilton, 1982.

Quick, T. *The Manager's Motivation Desk Book.* New York: Wiley, 1985.

Quick, T., and Higginson, M. "Sensitivity: The Missing Ingredient." *Advanced Management Journal,* Spring 1982.

Revel, J. *Without Marx or Jesus.* New York: Doubleday, 1971.

Roethlisberger, F., and Dickson, W. *Management and the Worker.* Cambridge, Mass.: Harvard University Press, 1939.

Sandburg, C. *Abraham Lincoln: The War Years.* San Diego: Harcourt, Brace, Jovanovich, 1954.

Tuchman, B. *The March of Folly: From Troy to Vietnam.* New York: Knopf, 1984.

Index